MIDLAND ENGLAND

BATSFORD BOOKS

1 A Northamptonshire Town, about 1800. *From a watercolour by John Varley*

THE FACE OF BRITAIN

MIDLAND ENGLAND

*A Survey of the Country
between the Chilterns
and the Trent*

By

W. G. HOSKINS

*Illustrated from photographs by
F. L. ATTENBOROUGH and others,
also from engravings and drawings*

B. T. BATSFORD LTD.
LONDON · NEW YORK · TORONTO · SYDNEY

Some men a forward motion love,
But I by backward steps would move

HENRY VAUGHAN (*The Silurist*)

First published, 1949

MADE AND PRINTED IN GREAT BRITAIN
BY JARROLD AND SONS LTD., NORWICH
FOR THE PUBLISHERS B. T. BATSFORD LTD.
LONDON: 15 NORTH AUDLEY STREET, W.1 AND MALVERN WELLS, WORCS.
NEW YORK: 122 EAST 55TH STREET   TORONTO: 480–6 UNIVERSITY AVENUE
SYDNEY: 156 CASTLEREAGH STREET

PREFACE

THIS book describes what is as a whole the most unknown and neglected part of England—the east midlands, the stretch of country from the Chilterns to the Trent. Apart from the hunting of Leicestershire and the churches of Northamptonshire, both long worshipped by their respective adherents, this midland country is ignored even by the intelligent traveller. It is merely a country of passage for him, on the way to points north, and few who are not natives feel tempted to leave the train or the car and explore this undistinguished countryside, which has no obvious charms and indeed much to repel at first sight from a main railway line.

There are books by the score about the Cotswolds and the Chilterns that bound the midland country on the south and south-west; about the "Shakespeare country" to the west and East Anglia on the other side; and the Pennines and the Peak that close it in on the north. But all these books skirt round and leave untouched the great tract of country in the middle of England. Everybody's geography is weakest when it comes to the midlands: rivers and towns are wildly misplaced, the counties are hard to remember by name and even more difficult to sort out clearly from each other. And yet because it is so solidly in the middle of England it is in some ways the most English of all the various provinces of this rich island; and I hope that something of this solid "Englishness" has come out in the pages that follow.

I am not a native of the midlands, but I have lived in them and explored them, mostly on foot, for the past sixteen years, apart from a sentence of nearly five years' imprisonment in London. But even that term of imprisonment, for such it must always be to any countryman, had its uses. Amid the deadly boredom and futility of life in London the only way to keep sane among the rootless millions of "countrymen on the road to sterility", as E. M. Forster has so truly described them, was to reflect on the years I had spent in walking through the midland fields and villages, coming home to search out in manuscripts and books the history of what I had seen during the day, and then out again to explore once more: the market-towns and villages, their churches and houses of all kinds, even the barns and the garden-walls, the fields and hedges; boring through the soil for villages buried long ago beneath the sheep-pastures, talking about the craftsmen of the past with their few surviving descendants. Far away in space and time from all this, an alien in London, I often reflected on how one could best convey the essential quality of the peaceful, quiet English midlands to anyone who did not know them, and this book is the result.

Whether or not I have succeeded in revealing something of the peculiar quality of this part of England I do not know. For my own part I am not much interested in surface impressions. The three visible dimensions of a building or a landscape are not enough: they may entrance for the moment but they make no abiding impression on the mind. One needs the fourth dimension of time to give depth to the scene: one wants to know as much as possible about the past life of a place, about its human associations, and to feel the long continuity of human life on that spot before it can make its full impression on the mind. Even a hedge far out in the fields may have a long history, going back to the great age of English colonisation of woodland and waste in the twelfth or thirteenth century, and the way it runs and the way it is constructed will tell of its origin. The smallest pool or spring far away from the village will have an ancient name that, could we but know it, illuminates its special quality today; the name over the village-shop may be one that is written in Domesday Book (perhaps even older than that): there are depths beyond depths in the simplest scene.

The midland countryside is not peculiar in this: the whole of the English landscape is a manuscript written on again and again, a palimpsest with endless discoveries waiting to be made; and one can learn, with sufficient patience, skill, and imagination, how to decipher this manuscript and make it yield its hidden meaning, though there will always be some detail, in the most well-known scene, that defies certainty. It is in this way, broadly, that I have chosen to interpret Midland England in this book, by showing how it has grown and what forces have moulded and shaped its landscapes and woven the pattern of its towns and villages. Much that I would have liked to say, much detail that would perhaps have made the rich pattern clearer to the mind, I have been obliged to forgo saying for want of space. But I hope I shall be able to say it at greater length on another occasion.

Leicester,
Autumn 1948

W. G. HOSKINS

THE MAIN GATES AT SCRAPTOFT HALL, NEAR LEICESTER, BY
WILLIAM EDNEY, *c.*1704
[*From the drawing by Alfred H. Hind*]

CONTENTS

ACKNOWLEDGMENT

I wish particularly to thank Mr. F. L. Attenborough for his photographs, which form the bulk of the illustrations to this book. These were all specially taken, in the course of many journeys, in order to illustrate the text, and a great deal of thought and patience has gone into each one. It is a matter for regret that so many others of equal excellence had to be discarded for reasons of space. And I wish to acknowledge his great help also in getting me to remote places all over the Midlands which I might not otherwise have been able to see in these difficult days.

In addition to the photographs by Mr. F. L. Attenborough the Publishers wish to thank the following photographers whose work is reproduced in these pages. The late Percy Bedford for Fig. 87; Mr. J. Allan Cash for Fig. 100; the Central Office of Information for Figs. 8, 96; the late B. C. Clayton for Figs. 19, 29, 39, 51, 60; Country Life Limited for Figs. 49, 54, 80; Mr. H. Felton for Figs. 3, 36, 44; Fox Photos Limited for Fig. 101; Mr. A. F. Kersting for Fig. 41; the late T. E. Routh for Fig. 73; Sport and General Photos Limited for Fig. 6; Topical Press Agency Limited for Figs. 5, 58; Raphael Tuck Limited for Figs. 4, 20, 38, 40, 107.

Thanks are also due to Mr. Edmund Blunden for permission to reproduce part of his poem "Forefathers", on page 61; to Mr. Albert Herbert for the drawings on page 115; to Mr. Alfred H. Hind for the drawing on page vi; and to the late Basil Oliver for the illustration on page viii. The frontispiece is reproduced by courtesy of the Squire Gallery, London, and the endpaper maps were specially drawn by Mr. Alfred L. Jones.

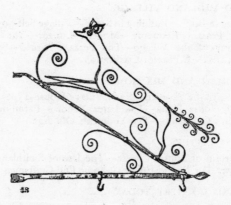

EIGHTEENTH-CENTURY WROUGHT-IRON DEVICE ONCE AT 'THE FOX,' HUNTINGDON, NOW IN THE VICTORIA AND ALBERT MUSEUM, SOUTH KENSINGTON

[*From the drawing by Basil Oliver, F.R.I.B.A.*]

2 Fotheringhay Church from across the Nene, Northamptonshire:
early fifteenth century

3   A Bedfordshire landscape at Eggington, near Stanbridge

4   The Southern Wall of the Midlands: the Chilterns, looking to Ivinghoe
Beacon

I

THE MIDLAND SCENE

AS the north-bound train breaks through the encircling band
of chalk round London, leaving behind at last the suburban
sprawl of the metropolis, it gathers speed across the green
pastures of Central England and the traveller settles down to endure
what seem to him the dull and featureless Midlands, where one
county shades unnoticeably into another every few miles so that he
never knows at any given moment which one he is in of the half-
dozen counties that fill the centre of the coloured map of England.
The landscape of green sloping pastures, of thin hedgerows and
small streams, spinneys and distant spires, unrolls endlessly the same
to his unpractised eye, only broken now and then by an even duller
little manufacturing town, smokeless, glowing with red brick, street
after street of late Victorian and Edwardian villas, and then on again
past the allotments and the cemetery into the green fields once more.
If he is slightly sensitive, the traveller will feel the train climbing
vigorously at times, though there are no conspicuous hills anywhere
to be seen, and sliding rapidly down long slopes to cross a slow,
muddy river whose name he will not know (is it, he wonders
vaguely, the Ouse, or the Nene or the Welland?); and then the train
comes suddenly out of a short tunnel and rolls clanking over the
broad and shining Trent, about which there is no doubt. The landscape changes suddenly now: stone walls blackened by industrial
dirt replace the hawthorn hedges of the past two hours, pit-head
gear and slag-heaps come into view more and more frequently, the
air in the carriage is perceptibly colder and fresher, voices on station
platforms are harder and speak in a strange tongue. We are across
the Trent, and this is the North. The traveller stirs from his
torpor and takes more notice of the outer world and its strange-
ness if he is a southerner; or, if he is a man from the north, he
recognises the familiar signs of home however much farther he
has to go. He has crossed the Great Divide between the south and
the north.

From the Chilterns (4) in the south to the crossing of the Trent between Derby and Nottingham is a stretch of eighty miles: this is Midland England, bounded sharply on the south by the high chalk escarpment and equally sharply on the north by the wide Trent as it comes "canking slow" around the foot of the Pennines. Eastwards the boundary is hardly less decisive: it is where the low clay ridges meet the endless sea of the fenland plain, and the Great North Road between Baldock and Newark roughly marks the division: fens to the east and midlands to the west, though we need not follow the road too blindly. Alconbury Hill, just north of Huntingdon, marks the precise boundary at that point. Though well under two hundred feet above the sea, it commands an apparently limitless expanse of fenland eastwards, glimmering beyond the reach of sight; and westwards one looks over the soft outlines of placid Huntingdonshire to the far-away smoke of Corby (107), in the next county, the iron heart of the Midlands.

This is the eastern frontier; but on the west it is harder to draw a defensible boundary. I would draw a fairly direct line from Burton on the Trent down to Oxford on the Thames, following the watershed between Trent and Avon and coming down the Cherwell, beyond which the West Country begins, leaving the whole of Shakespeare's country to the west, outside the Midlands. This is quite indefensible except on the good ground that Warwickshire and its neighbours, and Shakespeare's country in particular, have been written about so much, and so well, and are so familiar to all who care for the English scene at all, that I do not want to add unnecessary words. I want to speak of the unknown Midland country that lies between here and the fens, fifty miles away, the most generally unknown tract of country of any size in the whole of England. It includes the whole of five counties (Leicestershire, Rutland, Northamptonshire, Huntingdonshire, Bedfordshire) and all that part of Buckinghamshire that lies to the north of the chalk escarpment (and none of that horrible suburban mess that lies to the south); and on the north those parts of Derbyshire and Nottinghamshire that fall this side of the Trent. And lastly, that north-eastern corner of Oxfordshire, between the Chilterns and the Cherwell, which contains so much that is worth looking at.

This great stretch of country—large for England, at least—has a unity of its own. It is, or was up to 1939, very largely a landscape of green pastures, and of some of the finest pastures and fox-hunting country in the world; of gently undulating claylands broken by the three big Midland valleys, claylands that rarely stand six hundred feet above the sea but rise and fall in long slopes between two and three hundred feet up. In Defoe's day these clays were villainous: after passing Dunstable, he says—

5   At Rockingham Castle

6   In Rockingham Park, Northamptonshire

THE WOODLAND PYTCHLEY

7   A Midland landscape in summer: Seagrave, Leicestershire

"You enter the deep clays, which are so surprisingly soft, that it is perfectly frightful to travellers, and it has been the wonder of foreigners, how, considering the great number of carriages which are continually passing with heavy loads, those ways have been made practicable; indeed the great number of horses every year kill'd by the excess of labour in those heavy ways, has been such a charge to the country, that new building of causeways, as the Romans did of old, seems to me to be a much easier expence:

"From Hockley to Northampton, thence to Harborough, and Leicester, and thence to the very bank of the Trent, these terrible clays continue. . . ."

But it is not all clay. Across the Midlands from south-west to north-east runs the great oolitic escarpment, the Stone Belt, continuation of the Cotswolds through the Northampton Uplands and the uplands of east Leicestershire to Lincoln Edge; and these hills, which rarely form a sharp escarpment in the midland country, sometimes overtop seven hundred feet. Their highest point is Whatborough Hill in the Leicestershire Uplands (755 feet), said to be the highest ground until one reaches the borders of Asia. In this hill-country, partly isolated summits and partly a high tableland in places, the wind blows hard and cold and the very names of the villages show it—Cold Ashby, Cold Newton, Cold Overton, all in these hills. Up at Naseby, next door to Cold Ashby (Naseby used to be thought in the eighteenth century the very top of England and I have met Midland villagers who still think so) their voices are louder than anywhere else: they shout at each other to overcome that winter wind, when "huge uproar lords it wide".

Apart from this belt of oolitic limestone, with its accompanying ironstone or marlstone, stone that gives to not a few Midland towns and villages a beauty unsurpassed by the most over-written Cotswold places, the Charnwood district in West Leicestershire has the topmost height of all the Midlands in Bardon Hill (912 feet), with a superb view over the whole of central England.

Mostly, though, the Midlands are green, quiet country, and there is a characteristic Midland landscape that is known by heart to hunting people above all: pastures enclosed by low hawthorn hedges (rarely any other sort of fence, for the sake of the hunting); regular fields that run down to small streams flowing bank-high, muddy and eddying, in winter, and that rise up the farther slopes to a skyline crowned by a thin spinney or a line of great elms; roads running for the most part clean and straight with wide grass verges and lined with young ash trees. The ash and the elm are the great trees of the Midlands. It is a quiet kind of country under a winter sky, produced almost entirely by the planning of the Stuart and Georgian country houses and their noble parks, a common sight in this part of England, and by the parliamentary enclosures of George III's time, with their regular, ordered planning of fields and roads. Streams lined with stumpy pollarded willows, soft grey skies, views into the next county; spires piercing the horizon every mile or so all round—visible evidence of a once-populous and prosperous countryside; lapwings silently congregated in bleached pastures or in the rare fields of coffee-coloured ploughland: such are the Midlands in winter.

In summer, the Midland landscape can hardly be surpassed for richness of colour and scent. The broad herded meadows of the Welland (15), the Nene, and the Ouse, lie knee-deep in buttercups and cowslips, a golden carpet miles long, and the rising ground back from the valleys is dense with hawthorn. The heavy warm scent of the may-blossom is everywhere on the summer wind; cuckoos call incessantly from one spinney after another; the magpie planes silently down from the covert edge "like a note in music"; swallows skim the placid river-surfaces and finches and multitudes of other small birds dart in and out of the thick security of the hawthorn hedges. Old stone-slated roofs are bright with mosses and lichens; limestone walls shine like silver and the ironstone glows with a golden light; and long after the sun has gone down after a day of high summer these stone walls radiate a gentle heat as one passes by them in the evening, on coming late into some old town like Stamford or Oundle or Olney.

I said a moment ago that this landscape, as we see it today, was produced almost entirely by the country houses and the parliamentary enclosures fostered by them, but this is to view it superficially. For underneath this obvious pattern is that of a far older England before the days of Georgian enclosures: the broach spires of the thirteenth and fourteenth centuries speak of it, and the little manor-houses of Plantagenet and Tudor days, and so, too, do the stone-built farmhouses and cottages of the Elizabethan and Stuart countrymen. Even the fields, beneath their regular eighteenth-century pattern, tell of it, for they lie mostly in ridge and furrow and these markings are the visible traces of the strip-system of the old open fields. Here and there we can still trace the green balks or headlands that gave a way into the fields, and by walking over them detect how the old fields were planned. I think it may be possible one day to reconstruct the medieval fields of a midland village by walking over its modern fields in this way, observing all the signs and clues, but we are only just beginning to learn how to do this. That great historian, Maitland, said once that the Ordnance map of England was the finest document we have of its history, could we but learn how to decipher it. This is even more true of the landscape itself which, to those who have eyes to see and ears to hear, speaks everywhere of the life of the past.

The quality of the Midland counties cannot be apprehended from a speeding train or a car. The traveller out of St. Pancras or Euston, or along the road to Derby (A.6), sees them at their dullest. The traveller from Marylebone, that quiet backwater among the London termini, fares better, but even he misses nearly everything that is good. One must walk, or cycle, or use a car with great restraint if at all, to enjoy what Midland England has to offer—preferably walk. For though there is a typical Midland landscape, there is, too, a real diversity of scenery in every one of the Midland counties that only a slow approach will discover. It is not a countryside that shows its beauty flamboyantly like Devon or in long sweeping lines like the downland counties, but one of intimate little corners, away from the through-lines of traffic, that must be explored slowly and revisited again and again to know their charm. Even little Rutland has two entirely different faces; the airy limestone uplands to the north with their characteristic silver-grey stone villages and walls and far views; and the close, tumbled country of sudden little hills, of orchards and thick hedges and golden ironstone, in the south towards the Welland.

Leicestershire is just as strikingly divided between east and west: the west as dull as anything that England can show, almost level claylands as far as the eye reaches, broken by ugly little factory-villages of red brick, and the east a landscape of sharp hills, woodland, stone-built villages and many fine churches, all because there is stone underfoot and not a hundred-foot thickness of clay. And as for Charnwood Forest, there is nothing quite like it elsewhere in England, a triassic landscape rising untamed out of the most conventional countryside one could imagine.

Down in Northamptonshire there is the great contrast between the cold uplands of ironstone round Naseby and Daventry and the warm, park-like, tree-studded lower country, and in Huntingdonshire, to the east, the contrast between the great water-meadows and the clay uplands. Along the wide valley of the Ouse there is a sense of water everywhere, even when one cannot see it: the willows, the level meadows, the great skies that begin to resemble those of fenland not far away to the east, the sound of creaking oars behind hedges, and the smell of the river. It is all in soft colours, greys and greens, and one understands immediately why England produced a school of water-colours.

Away from the Ouse and its feeders, Huntingdonshire is a landscape of low ridges rising gently to the horizon a mile or two away, of far corn-coloured views, of distant clumps of trees and beautiful spires rising suddenly out of them, as along the Thrapston–Huntingdon road.

Buckinghamshire is even more markedly divided between north

and south: the south almost swamped by the suburban tide out of London which is washing now against Aylesbury (97), nearly forty miles out; and to the north, the almost unknown claylands with their fine parks, unspoilt villages, pleasant little churches, and old manor-houses away from it all. And to the east lies unknown Bedfordshire, which suffers more than any other of the Midland shires from being seen from a main-line railway that traverses its dullest parts—Luton, Bedford, brickworks and suburban building. And yet along the Great Ouse and its tributaries the valleys are full of charming villages and quietly beautiful English scenery, while to the south runs the greensand ridge by Woburn and Ampthill, "a strip of land", says Mr. Arnold Palmer, whose words I cannot but quote, "rich in natural and architectural beauties and rare literary associations. It links the Cowper country (above the Brickhills) and the John Bunyan country—not only the places where they lived but the scenes which again and again were the inspiration and matter of their writings. In the history of our literature, this corridor of fifteen miles is unsurpassed in sanctity, in peculiar purity."

There is variety and diversity in all the Midland counties, however uniformly green and pastoral they may seem to those who cannot see anything that is not flamboyant or highly coloured. Nowhere is the midland scene magnificent or brilliant or exciting; but except for western Leicestershire and small parts of Bedfordshire, which are irredeemably dull, it is satisfying to the mind and sometimes much more. There is, for example, the green deserted country round Knaptoft in the south of Leicestershire, where the pastures of central England hardly touch five hundred feet above the sea and yet they are the watershed between Trent and Severn; and streams gather here that end in the Humber, the Wash, and the Bristol Channel. This, more than anywhere, is the very heart of England: Knaptoft, with its ruined church, its font under the trees, its village under the sheep-pastures since Henry VII's time, its medieval manor-house marked only by a rectangular island within a drying moat, and the later Elizabethan hall itself falling into slow ruin at the top of the field. Once full of life, a thriving village of plough-land and meadow in the thirteenth century, the squire within his moat and the parson in the newly built church, now it dreams its life away in the autumn sunshine, deserted by all save occasional blackberry-pickers.

The valleys of the three great Midland rivers are not unlovely at any time of the year, especially Welland and Ouse. The Welland, most northerly of them, breaks out from its natal hills at Market Harborough and, though many more miles pass before it becomes a noticeable river, flows through a spacious valley, two miles or so across, so wide that even on the bordering slopes one can hardly detect the course of the little stream through the meadows. The

8   Summer Ploughing in Northamptonshire

9 Winter floods in the Midlands: the Soar near Hathern, Leicestershire

views from the southern or Northamptonshire hillside are generally fine. This is a long ridge of ground some two or three hundred feet above the broad meadows, crowned by a series of good churches with bold spires—Dingley, Brampton Ash, Stoke Albany, Wilbarston, and Cottingham. All along this ridge there are views across the valley over to the Leicestershire hills (15), best of all from the road half-way between Cottingham and Rockingham, from which one looks northward far into Leicestershire and Rutland, great blue distances, and nearer at hand sees the sun shining on the handsome limestone spires of Great Easton (Leicestershire) and Caldecott (Rutland); and well down the valley the impressive viaduct of the London Midland and Scottish railway leaps over the whole width in a series of towering arches. Close to, this viaduct is a monstrous and hideous affair, with nothing to be said for it except its impressiveness as these things go in England. But seen from a few miles away, softened by distance, and best of all perhaps from the road that crosses the valley between Wakerley and Barrowden three miles below, it gives an almost Italian character to the whole view, especially if the light has that misty bloom that one so often gets in late summer.

The Welland valley is most attractive all the way from Market Harborough down to Stamford, where it enters the fens, and it is lined on either side by excellent stone-built villages, some of them lovely indeed, with handsome churches. On the Leicestershire side are Bringhurst and Great Easton, and Hallaton a little way back, all most attractive; and in Rutland are Caldecott and Liddington, Barrowden, Ketton (27), and Tinwell. And so we reach lovely Stamford with its spires and towers and coloured mansard roofs, the "stone-ford" over the Welland and the crown of the whole valley.

On the Northamptonshire side almost every village is a pleasure to look at, full of seventeenth- and eighteenth-century farmhouses and cottages, the great period of country building all over the Midlands. Most beautiful of all is little Rockingham (69), with its single street climbing gently southwards up the hill, curving at the same time and so leading the eye up to that royal castle that towers over it all. The castle, founded by William the Conqueror on an older earthwork that dominated the valley, is superbly sited on the lip of the high ground where it falls steeply down to the Welland, two hundred feet below, governing the valley up and down for miles just as Belvoir does in an even grander way on its own escarpment overlooking the distant Trent. Belvoir must be, next to Windsor, the grandest castle-site in England; but Rockingham, with its two drum-towers looking massively outwards (5), is hardly less imposing from across the valley.

Continuing down the valley we come to Gretton, Harringworth, and Wakerley, all good in their various ways: and then we arrive at Duddington (71, 76), the loveliest of the limestone villages as Rockingham is of the ironstone, with a fine old mill on the river, a highly interesting church, and streets of beautiful country building. But a little way on, and up on the high ground, is Duddington's equal—Colly Weston (70), the home of the famous stone-slates that have roofed castles and cottages in these parts since the fourteenth century. I would put Colly Weston and Duddington above many of the Cotswold villages as architectural masterpieces.

Beyond lies Easton-on-the-Hill, a large and attractive village with an ancient rectory built about 1500, a most interesting and complete example of late medieval architecture. Here we are in sight of Stamford again, and so, passing the ruins of Wothorpe (we are now entering the visible domain of the Cecils of Burghley), we come down into the town, crossing the bridge that has been here since Henry II's days. Straight ahead, at the top of the sharp hill leading up from the bridge, is the superb tower and spire of St. Mary's, to which Sir Walter Scott always bared his head when he made the journey along the Great North Road from London to Scotland, as the finest sight on the whole road.

This stretch of the Welland valley, the twenty-two miles from Harborough to Stamford, is full of fine spreading views from the hillside roads, of rich farming land and lovely meadow scenery, of excellent villages and handsome churches, all along both sides. Whoever spends a day travelling down one side of the valley, the second day in Stamford, and returns on the third along the other side has had a banquet of the eye and mind.

The Nene Valley is not so uniformly attractive as the Welland. Its middle course is through a messy landscape, the product of the Victorian boot and shoe industry, which has sprinkled wide stretches of country from Northampton down to Thrapston with shapeless red-brick townships and villages. This district is only to be visited for its notable churches—Earl's Barton, with the best Anglo-Saxon tower in the country, Higham Ferrers (26), Raunds, Irchester, Irthlingborough, and Stanwick; all closely grouped together in the industrial mess. In the same small piece of country, there are Whiston (29), one of the most handsome village churches in England; St. Peter's, Northampton, magnificent late Norman work, and the Renaissance church of All Saints, built after the fire of 1675; and not least, the most notable modern church of St. Mary at Wellingborough, a blaze of colour internally.

But it is below Thrapston that the Nene valley achieves its full beauty of landscape and of architecture, culminating in the Oundle district. From Thrapston down to Oundle there are excellent lime-

10   The Ouse at Hemingford Grey, Huntingdonshire

11 Summer in the Midland Pastures: King's Norton, Leicestershire

stone villages of the best Northamptonshire type along both banks of the river, generally with fine churches also. Lowick and Titchmarsh are just on the fringes of the valley: both villages are excellent and their churches are notable even for Northamptonshire—lovely examples of Perpendicular building in its latest and greatest days (25, 30). The Aldwinkles and the Barnwells are good also, on either side of the valley, and then there is Wadenhoe with its curiously isolated little church up on a hill above the river. There are signs that the original village was near the church, as we should expect, but for some reason it seems to have moved later *en bloc* some distance away. There are many such tantalising problems in medieval archaeology in the Midlands.

Polebrook has an outstandingly interesting thirteenth-century church, full of good detail even for the layman's eye; and so we come to Oundle, which, like Fotheringhay, should always be approached from the south for the first time. Oundle is one of the most beautiful towns in England, only inferior to Stamford because it has not the wealth of medieval building that Stamford has. Its grey streets of seventeenth-century houses, with their lichened uneven roofs of Colly Weston slates and their characteristic succession of bay-windows, dormers, and gables, reach their best in the two great inns—the Talbot (1626) and the even better White Lion (1641) (94). The numerous eighteenth-century houses are most handsome and even more pleasing: less "picturesque" than the Carolean houses in St. Osyth's Lane perhaps, but more satisfying as architecture. The whole length of North Street is an architectural feast, ranging in date from the first decades of the seventeenth to the first decades of the nineteenth century, two centuries of the finest English building in stone. And above it all soars the magnificent tower and spire of the parish church, two hundred feet above the roofs and the meadows.

One should walk along the meadows of the Nene below Oundle on a summer evening. Behind, the spire of Oundle soars above the little town, silhouetted against the southern sky, and ahead, two or three miles away, the lantern-tower of Fotheringhay (2), a masterpiece of fifteenth-century architecture, rises from its enclosing trees. Ahead also, and on the other side of the meadows, rises the spire of Warmington church, that unforgettable monument of thirteenth-century craftsmanship in stone. Over the river the light fades on Cotterstock and Tansor (77), the mill, the churches, and the grey stone houses across the wide meadows: the summer evening light in the water-meadows and the silhouettes of lovely towers and spires all round the landscape. And so one goes on through beautiful villages, through Nassington (63) to Wansford, on the Great North Road, where one can either continue northwards into Stamford once

c

more or turn eastward past the fine Norman church of Castor into Peterborough, with its great abbey church that is now the finest cathedral by far in the Midlands.

The valley of the Great Ouse, one of England's largest rivers, for it is a hundred and fifty miles long, is the most pastoral and quiet of all the midland valleys, with its charming villages all through Buckinghamshire, Bedfordshire, and Huntingdonshire, sprinkled beside the wide, level meadows, and its succession of pleasant little market towns—Buckingham, Stony Stratford, Newport Pagnell, Olney, St. Neots, Huntingdon (17, 93), and St. Ives (14, 16), where we enter the fens. Wolverton is the only real blot, a typical railway town, and Bedford (96) is its largest lapse from pure country. The Welland valley is without industrial stain and in this respect is superior to the Ouse: but the Ouse in its country reaches is a nobler stream, with some of the loveliest river and meadow scenery in the whole of England. And as one should follow the Welland along its length from Harborough to Stamford, so one should meander with the Ouse in its great sweeping curves from Buckingham down to Bedford and from Bedford on to Huntingdon and St. Ives, cutting across and getting away from the Midland traffic streams, which flow diagonally across the valleys and not along them.

Below Huntingdon are some of the prettiest villages in the Midlands. The Ouse moves, for *flows* is not the word to describe its progress, through wide, willow-lined meadows, past Houghton and the Hemingford to St. Ives. Houghton (62), on the northern bank, is full of the tiled and mansard or hipped roofs that are characteristic of this attractive little county, bright with mosses and lichens, gardens full of brilliant colour, walls washed in cream or ochre, doors of brilliant blues, greens, and reds. There is no suburban timidity about colour in Huntingdonshire: none of that dreary preference for "sensible" colours like sludge-brown or slug-grey. Houghton has black and white timber-framed houses also, and thatched and whitewashed cottages of later date; but its great mill is now only a youth hostel, a museum piece, not a living, working centre of village economy: one of the many symptoms of England's decay which we encounter over and over again in the countryside.

Across the river from Houghton are the Hemingfords—Hemingford Abbots and Hemingford Grey—both astonishingly pretty to look at. Hemingford Abbots is brilliant with colour (peach, cream, white, black, blues, reds, and greens), much excellent thatching elaborately patterned, and some good tarred and timbered barns. Hemingford Grey (10), a mile farther on, is even better: it must be one of the show villages of England, full of black and white timbered houses of Elizabethan and Jacobean times, of other good seventeenth-century building, and some lovely Queen Anne and early Georgian

12   Willen Church, Buckinghamshire, designed by Robert Hooke,
1679–80

13   Village building at Sulgrave, Northamptonshire

14   The Ouse at St. Ives, Huntingdonshire

building in red brick near the river. There is even a Norman manor-house near by, one of the best examples of twelfth-century domestic architecture in the country.

South of the Ouse valley one should still travel at right angles to the main lines of traffic, following the axis of the greensand ridge and plateau of which I have already spoken, with its characteristic and beautiful scenery of woodland and natural heath, rising to over five hundred feet in places and leading one on across the border into Buckinghamshire. All the way along, the bold line of the Chiltern escarpment closes the view to the south, the southern wall of the midland park (4).

We cross into the northern parts of Buckinghamshire, as unknown for the most part as the southern half is overrun, where there is much pleasant country, many attractive villages, and satisfying churches and manor-houses. Ahead lie the market-towns of Aylesbury (97), Buckingham, and Winslow, all delightful places to saunter round, but especially the last two: little red-brick and stucco towns of the most contented and reposeful period in English history.

Just beyond Aylesbury, over the Oxfordshire border, is Thame, another beautiful little town, hardly touched as yet by the twentieth century's clumsy hands. Thame is difficult to get at: its "transport facilities" are bad: and so it remains a delight to the eye. Aylesbury, however, is at one end of the suburban train service from the inferno of Baker Street and is being ruined by the contact, though it has a good deal of seemly Georgian building in its more secluded streets.

Both Aylesbury and Thame are built mostly of old brick, with much good stucco, but farther north one comes on to the stone once more. Brackley (92) is a pleasant little country town; Banbury (103) has much excellent building in stone of the best periods, and is in the midst of country that is notable for lovely villages and striking churches—Adderbury and Deddington, just away from the Cher-well, Bloxham with a lovely church in the local style of North Oxfordshire, and Great Tew, a perfect little village which is the result of single ownership at the great house, without any of the self-consciousness of a show-place. But Great Tew is on its way out, like so many other villages that were once prosperous and beautiful: where there were once twenty men on the estate to keep it in good order, now there are only four.

Here, however, we are six hundred feet up in the foothills of the Cotswolds; Chipping Norton is only four or five miles away; and we are at the frontiers of our midland territory. There is much else one could say about the midland landscape, its towns and villages (not all so commendable by a long way) and its rivers and hills, houses and churches; but all this will emerge in its proper place.

II

THE PEOPLING OF THE MIDLANDS

THE early history of the Midlands is dominated by its great rivers, and chiefly the three that empty into the Wash, that deep bay facing the continent from which nearly all our ancestors have come in the past four thousand years. The rivers explain the pre-history of the Midlands; they are the ways by which the earliest settlers moved. And they are even more striking in their influence when we come to the great Anglo-Saxon invasions from the fifth century onwards. To the Romans, with their military road-system, engineered *across* the midland river-valleys (and not along them) like the nineteenth-century railways, the rivers were of no consequence; but we see their influence again, long after the Anglo-Saxon settlement, in the way they were used for carrying building stone in medieval times to districts otherwise stoneless, so giving us noble parish churches far away from the famous Northampton-shire quarries. In talking of the peopling of the Midlands, then, we are continually brought back to the four rivers—Trent, Welland, Nene, and Ouse—by which nearly all the early peoples came in. Only the Romans did not: but their permanent influence in this part of England was very slight and can soon be dismissed.

Midland England was largely a great tract of clays, under various names—boulder clay, Oxford clay, Liassic clay—but all heart-breaking, cold and heavy, and densely forested under natural condi-tions. So it is that on the map of Neolithic Britain the middle of England is almost a blank space, and even on the Bronze Age Map (1900–500 B.C.), they are only thinly spotted with evidence of human occupation. Such evidence as there is clusters together in highly localised areas, on the "dry-soil" patches of the oolitic limestone mostly, and close to the rivers. The open or lightly wooded heath country around the upper Witham, where Lincolnshire and Leices-tershire meet on high ground, shows much Bronze Age settlement, and the isolated Charnwood Forest district also stands out on a distribution-map. The largest clusters are, however, in the Peterborough district, where the Nene enters the fens, and on the eastward slopes of the Northamptonshire uplands which drain down into the Nene. Sir Cyril Fox shows (in *The Personality of Britain*) that Bronze Age man favoured this combination of conditions for his settlements: in the Midlands, not on the top of the dry-soil uplands as we might expect, but on the lower slopes nearest to rivers or streams, so that his flocks could pasture freely on the slopes and he himself had fresh water, fish, and fowl from the rivers. The rivers, too, were important channels of trade from the Late Bronze Age onwards (1000–500 B.C.) and two of the three largest dug-out boats found in Britain have come from the midland rivers—from Deeping Fen by the Welland, and Warboys (Huntingdonshire), between Ouse and Nene. The age of these boats is not certainly known, but they probably indicate long-distance river traffic before the Bronze Age was out.

This traffic along the rivers was a further reason for settlement on the dry gravel terraces beside them, and we have local clusters of Bronze Age finds along the middle reaches of all the larger midland rivers. The men of the Bronze Age were already selecting the sites where medieval towns later grew (like Peterborough on the Nene and Leicester on the Soar), where land-traffic could cross the river most easily from one gravel terrace to the other, and where river-traffic similarly found its first good landing-place. It seems likely, too, that the well-marked prehistoric trackway that for twelve miles forms the boundary between Leicestershire and Lincolnshire, originated in the late Bronze Age (if not a little earlier) as an overland link between the Welland and the Trent, across the high limestone plateau. It seems to have gone from Stamford (or "the stone ford", where Stamford later grew) right across to Newark.

But for all these interesting local evidences of human occupation in the Bronze Age, the fact remains that the Midlands were uninhabited over vast stretches of country, and only thinly peopled in little local clusters. Nor is it any different in the early Iron Age and right into Roman times.

The early Iron Age map (*c.* 500 B.C.–1st cent. A.D.) is perhaps even blanker than that of the Bronze Age. The hill-forts, which are such an impressive feature of this period in southern and western England, are rarely found in the Midlands, and in the main are not on a grand scale. Burrough Hill, seven hundred feet up on the marlstone escarpment of East Leicestershire, is a notable site; and Breedon Hill, an isolated block of limestone in North-west Leicestershire, is of the same date (probably 1st cent. B.C.–1st cent. A.D.). Hunsbury Camp, just outside Northampton, has been properly excavated and shows one kind of settlement that grew up among the midland forests. It showed traces of life back to the fourth century

B.C.; the earliest site probably had no fortifications and had been reached by the Nene; and it had probably been chosen because of the ironstone under the camp, for the great number of iron objects and the amount of slag found indicated that it was an iron-working site. The site was occupied for about four hundred years, but was deserted before the Roman conquest; perhaps the arrival of the Belgae at Duston, close by, ended the settlement in the first years of the Christian era. The inhabitants were agriculturists, tending cattle and growing grain; they hunted deer, made pottery, wove cloth, worked in bronze and in stone, mined and worked their own iron. It is very likely that Burrough Hill in Leicestershire, which has not yet been excavated, was a similar site, for it, too, lies on the ironstone, which was used to make the dry-walling of the ramparts. This dry-walling, seen and noted by Leland on his travels in Henry VIII's time, had long been covered by the short turf of this windy promontory, but Home Guard activities in the recent war have exposed it once again in several places.

The Roman occupation of the Midlands was never very extensive. Leicester (*Ratae Coritanorum*) was their largest town (105 acres) and the heart of this town with its basilica, shops, and public baths, has been laid bare in recent years among the factories and activity of the modern city, forming one of the largest areas of Roman building to be found anywhere in England. There was a double town, too, on the north and south banks of the Nene, where Ermine Street crossed the river. The southern town, now a deserted site near the village of Chesterton, covered about 44 acres, the northern (*Durobrivae*, now Castor) was of unknown extent. Together they were the centre of a remarkable pottery industry in this part of the Nene valley, producing the Roman Ware known as "Castor".

The only other Roman towns were small and unimportant. Towcester (68) and Irchester, both in Northamptonshire, covered 35 and 20 acres respectively; and Godmanchester (84), on the southern bank where Ermine Street crossed the Ouse, was a small market town whose exact extent is unknown.

The majority of the people of Roman Britain were, however, country-dwellers, living on large country estates or in the native villages; but here, too, with local exceptions, the Midlands did not attract people. There is a thin sprinkling of villas on the oolite in Northamptonshire and Rutland, but elsewhere in the Midlands they are scarce; and native villages are few. Roman roads drove through the Midlands on their way elsewhere: Ermine Street follows the eastern edge above the fens, Watling Street runs north-west from London, made as a penetrative road towards the lands of the yet unconquered Welsh, and the Fosse Way cuts diagonally from south-west to north-east across the country, constructed as a frontier road at the completion of one stage in the Roman conquest (*c.* A.D. 46–47). At High Cross (*Venonae*), the Fosse and Watling Streets crossed at right angles, on the watershed between Trent and Severn, a spot that might well be regarded as the very centre of England—certainly as the centre of Roman Britain.

But the people of the Midlands today have few ancestors among the pre-Roman and Roman inhabitants of their landscape: they are fundamentally a mixture of Angles, Saxons, and Danes with a distinct trace of Norwegian and a dash of Norman: here is the real English mixture. And it is here, in this part of England, in the early monasteries of the Nene valley, that the east Midland speech became the standard English tongue. Somewhere just north of Bedford, one crosses what is perhaps the most fundamental speech-barrier in this country, between those who pronounce their vowels after the southern manner and those who speak the northern way. Words like *bus* and *come* are test-words: in the south they say bŭs, cŭm, in the north bōōs, cōōm. At Bedford it is still the Saxon speech, but as his train draws up in Leicester station the exiled Yorkshireman can catch the unmistakable traces of his own speech and he feels that he is nearing home.

This invisible line in the heart of the Midlands, where the vowels change subtly from southern to northern, marks the racial division between the Angles and the Saxons, the two great Teutonic peoples who are usually lumped together indiscriminately: but it is strictly only in the southern Midlands, where they met and overlapped, that one can truthfully speak of "Anglo-Saxon", for elsewhere they are either Angles or Saxons, if they are English at all. So the Midland people are preponderantly Anglian north of the Ouse, Saxon south of it; but those to the north have been heavily crossed with Danish blood also. In the tenth and eleventh centuries it is probable that one half the inhabitants of Leicestershire were of Scandinavian descent, so that the Leicestershire mixture today is almost an equal proportion of Anglo-Scandinavian; but the Scandinavian influence as one goes south diminishes appreciably. It is still strong in Northamptonshire, and is probably more marked in Huntingdonshire, Bedfordshire, and North Buckinghamshire, than the local place-names would suggest. This Scandinavian blood is practically all Danish, but the Norwegians who crossed over from Ireland in the tenth century and settled thickly along our north-west coasts, trickled down into the northern Midlands and founded a few villages. There are five Normantons (i.e. *tun* of the Northmen, or Norwegians) in Nottinghamshire, three each in Leicestershire and Derbyshire and one in Rutland, and *Normancross* hundred in Huntingdonshire reveals their presence also. Frisians, from the islands off the Dutch and German coasts, settled in the Midlands also: there are

two Frisbys (Frisians' *by*) in Leicestershire, besides three villag
Lincolnshire whose names betray them (Friesthorpe, and
Friestons).

It was the Angles who first occupied the midland forests or
considerable scale, coming in by the Wash and the Humber
penetrating into the heart of England by the rivers that ros
back in that unknown land. By the Trent they reached the N
Midlands, and by its tributary the Soar they reached the hea
Leicestershire. The early history of Nottinghamshire centres o
Trent, that of Northamptonshire on the Nene, and of Bedford
and Huntingdonshire on the Ouse. Along the Welland, wh
mostly a boundary-river, the earliest Angles reached Rutland
south-east of Leicestershire (not touched by the Trent–Soar r
and the north-east of Northamptonshire, which was cut off from
the rest of the county by the great forest of Rockingham on the
plateau between Welland and Nene. Along the four valleys (Trent,
Welland, Nene, and Ouse) and their major tributaries the Angles of
the Migration Age came in considerable numbers and had reached
the farthest western watershed, beyond which lay the Avon-Severn
basin, by the year 500.

The Trent hardly lies within our province, except as a way in on
the north. Its importance in the earliest phase of the Anglo-Saxon
conquest is sufficiently borne out by the distribution of heathen
Anglian cemeteries along its valley,[1] and by the sites of the earliest
place-names, practically all of which are to be found close to or on
the river. Names ending in *-ing* and *-ingham* are now accepted as
being the oldest place-names in the English Conquest (subject to
the qualification that some place-names of this type today are
deceptive as they are corruptions of a less significant name), and
along the Trent we find Gedling, Meering, Nottingham, and
Hoveringham. Practically all the archaic place-names are on or near
the river, except Hickling which lies away to the south on the
Leicestershire border, but the hinterland of the valley, mostly heavy
clays, was not settled until an appreciably later period.

It is, however, by the three rivers that open into the Wash that
the main flood of Anglian settlers penetrated the Midlands, and of
these the Nene shows the most extensive traces of early settlements,
just as it showed most signs of life in the Bronze and Early Iron
Ages. But let us begin with the most northerly of the three valleys
—that of the Welland.

Down in the fens we find the archaic place-names of Spalding
and the Deepings, on the banks of the river; and Stamford, where

[1] The kingdom of the Middle Angles, which covered the greater part of the Midlands,
was converted to Christianity about the year 653. We may therefore roundly date all
the heathen cemeteries in the Midlands as before 650.

fenland fades away and the limestone uplands begin, has pro-
ed evidence of occupation at an early date in a primitive window-
. This can be dated as not later than A.D. 500, and possibly a
e earlier in the closing years of the fifth century. Just away from
Welland, up little side-valleys, we find Empingham and Upping-
n, in Rutland, and a little higher up the Welland itself, the two
cent villages of Rockingham and Cottingham. There are no
er recognisable archaic names to the west until we reach the
tlings, in the heart of Leicestershire, which must have been
led from the Welland valley; but a heathen cemetery at North
ffenham in Rutland has produced fifth-century evidence, and one
two sites in Leicestershire are hardly later than this. There is a
cinating little place close beside the Welland, in the south-eastern
up of Leicestershire on which something must be said. It is the
sequestered little village of Bringhurst, on the summit of an isolated
hill rising a hundred and fifty feet above the broad meadows of the
valley-bottom.

Even looking at it on the one-inch map it strikes anyone with a
nose for the remote past as a place worth going to inspect closely,
with its curious isolated round hill in that unexpected place, its
church perched right in the centre of the summit and the village
(such as it is) grouped closely in a ring round this ancient focus, the
whole place gathered tidily on a little plateau of a few acres in extent.
It smells of antiquity even on the map. And when one sees it from
the valley, one look is enough: that solid, squat church-tower,
planted firmly like a lighthouse on a rock, the circular churchyard,
the stone-built farmhouses and cottages ringed round it, the whole
scene quite unlike what one expects in the Midlands. From the top,
from any of those warm stone-walled gardens that run out behind
the farmhouses and cottages to the edge of the plateau, there are
great spacious blue views up and down the valley over the hills of
Rutland, Leicestershire, and Northamptonshire—an obvious site for
the earliest settlers in the valley. Opposite is the low grey fortress
of Rockingham on its answering hill and the bold spire of Cottingham rises from a typical huddle of houses: both are archaic place-
names, dating from c. A.D. 500. And when one pursues the matter
further, having seen the place, all one's suspicions are confirmed by
such written evidence as there is. The name itself is not recognisably
archaic: one could not unhesitatingly assign it to the earliest period
of the English Settlement: it is "the *hyrst* (the wooded knoll) of
Bryni's people"—*Bryninga-hyrst*. But we discover that it is, though
so small and remote today, the mother-church of a large area round
about, of places today much bigger than itself, that it was a royal
estate and was given to Peterborough Abbey as early as A.D. 700
by its royal owner and that it had a church in pre-Conquest times.

None of these things is conclusive in itself, but taking them all together they point to Bringhurst as the site of one of the earliest Anglian settlements on the Leicestershire side of the Welland, if not the earliest, and I would hazard the opinion that it had been founded at the same time as Rockingham and Cottingham across the meadows, by the end of the fifth century.

The uplands which separate the Welland and the Nene valleys were mostly forested country and were avoided by the earliest waves of invaders (though Benefield in the middle of this district may well be an early name), and it is in the main valley of the Nene that we find the most extensive traces of other early settlers. The whole of the valley from its source down to where it enters the Fens has produced heathen cemeteries and other finds in abundance, and teems with place-names of the remotest period of the Anglian conquest (Daventry, Naseby, Weedon, Oundle, Billing, to name only a few). By the late fifth century the immediate slopes of the Nene valley and its chief tributaries (like the Ise) had been occupied, but, as with the Trent, the claylands back from the river were left for a later and more gradual clearing and settlement which went on up to the eve of the Danish conquest in the late ninth century. In this valley, too, were founded two of the oldest monasteries in England —Medeshamstede and Oundle, both destroyed in the Danish Wars without leaving any traces. Oundle was never revived, but Medeshamstede took on a new life as Peterborough Abbey with the restoration of peace in the tenth century.

Between the Nene and the Ouse, too, stretched a great forest, part of which was called *Bruneswald* in the eleventh century, into the depths of which the outlaw Hereward retreated with his men. The village names of Newton Bromswold (Northamptonshire) and Leighton Bromswold (Huntingdonshire) commemorate this lost forest today, and the forests of Salcey and Whittlewood are meagre remnants of the whole.

Like the other valleys, that of the Ouse was the channel by which the first waves of invaders reached the depths of the south Midlands, until they were checked by the formidable forests on the western watershed of the region, like their fellows who pushed up Welland and Nene. On the whole, Bedfordshire, Huntingdonshire, and the northern half of Buckinghamshire were settled later, however, than Northamptonshire, the county to the north: place-names of an archaic type are fewer (cf., however, the Gidding country on the uninviting clay uplands bordering *Bruneswald*) and finds of archaic material are not so common. It is in the Ouse valley, in Bedfordshire, that the Angles who came up from the Wash in the earliest days met the West-Saxons pushing up from the south-west, giving that intermingling of Saxon and Anglian cultures and peoples

15　The Welland Valley, looking from the Northamptonshire slopes towards Great Easton, Leicestershire

16   The Medieval Bridge and chapel at St. Ives, Huntingdonshire:
early fifteenth century

17   Cutwaters of the Medieval Bridge at Huntingdon, *c.* 1370

that is revealed in the important heathen cemetery of Kempston in Bedfordshire.

From these scattered settlements in the main river valleys, occupied by the beginning of the sixth century for the most part, the work of colonisation went on up the slopes of the forested hills that separated the alluvial lands, though here and there hill-top sites had been occupied from the first (e.g. Whatborough and Bringhurst in Leicestershire, or Naseby in Northamptonshire) and the expansion here must have been downhill into the forest of the lower clays. In those generations after the first great migration, the noise of axe and saw and hammer was heard in the Midland woods year after year: timber came crashing down, stumps were rooted up, ditches dug, hedges made, and smoke rose slowly from new villages and hamlets among the trees. More and more of the stubborn midland clays were broken up, here and there (as at Brixworth and Breedon, Oundle and Repton) simple churches arose in the darkness of the seventh century, and swallows began to find their way summer after summer to barns and stables hitherto unknown.

The great majority of these villages were founded in the Midlands at the spring-line where a pervious soil rests on an impervious. Two hundred of Northamptonshire's 290 hamlets, villages, and towns had their beginnings in this way, forty were perched on hill-tops (and many of these must be the oldest villages in their own district) and fifty were down in the valley-bottom, mostly on the river-gravels. Some of the latter, too, like Oundle, go back to the earliest days of the English settlement. In Leicestershire we find much the same thing, and no doubt it is true of the other Midland counties, which I have not looked at so closely.

For ten or twelve generations this hard but peaceful work went on in the countryside, and the great open fields that are so characteristic of the Midland landscape year by year pushed back the encircling forest a little farther; and then in the middle years of the ninth century there came to these inland settlers dim rumours of a peril from across the same sea as that on which their ancestors had rolled towards their new homes. The Danes were attacking the English coasts and every year their violence grew. Soon even the midland countryside was being ravaged by war, the monasteries of the Nene valley went up in flames, and many an isolated little village perished unknown in the struggle. With the establishment of peace, the peace between Alfred and Guthrum, most of the Midlands—all that to the north and east of Watling Street, which became the frontier of the Danish empire—was parcelled out among the various Danish armies who settled on the land, took over old villages and gave them a new name, and founded many new ones. Though they retained their military organisation for long afterwards, they probably lived peacefully enough side by side with the English they had conquered, for, after all, farming cannot be carried on in an open-field community except on a completely co-operative basis.

Though much of Danish England had been recaptured by the English within forty or fifty years, the partition of Mercia among the Danish host made an indelible mark upon the Midlands, less so in the south than in the part beyond Watling Street. The map of Leicestershire is thickly studded with Scandinavian village-names (for example, there are no fewer than fifty-eight names ending in *by* alone), and though the counties to the south show this impress much less obviously it comes out strongly in the minor names of the landscape (especially the old field-names) of Northamptonshire and elsewhere. The names of the streets in some of the Midland towns reveal the same influence to this day (e.g. the frequent use of *gate* for "street" in Leicester and Loughborough), and over the little shops in back streets and on the boards over the inn or pub door one reads good old Scandinavian names that are scarcely disguised after a thousand years—Astill, Herrick, Gamble, Chettle, Tookey, Nutt, Swain and many more. How many of these little shopkeepers in the towns, or obscure farmers in the villages, could, if they but knew, boast of a descent of a thousand years, putting a Norman pedigree to shame.

The old speech of Midland England was full, too, of outlandish words that were pure Scandinavian and of hard sounds that betrayed another tongue than English, *thakking* for thatching, *ligging* for lying; and in every county there are still villages whose speech has been regarded as strange and barbaric by their neighbours for centuries.

There is no doubt that Danish was a spoken language in certain parts of Leicestershire and Northamptonshire, at least, for many generations, perhaps for some centuries. In the open market-place of Leicester, probably held in the same place in the tenth century as it is in the twentieth, Danish must have been heard as often as Old English, for most of the villages round the town were predominantly Danish in their population even as late as the closing years of the eleventh century.

The Scandinavian settlement left its mark in less obvious ways also. It seems certain that the present boundaries of most of the Midland counties, drawn as they are around a central town and called after that town, were demarcated in the early tenth century as the territories of particular Danish armies which "obeyed" the shire town. We know that Northamptonshire owes its origin to this Danish military organisation, and Leicestershire is just as obviously another example. Lincolnshire, Huntingdonshire, and Bedfordshire, all named after and drawn around a central town—the *burh* to which an army answered—doubtless arose in this way also.

And lastly, the settlement of several thousands of military men on the land in the Midlands, on land granted to them freehold (as we should say in modern language), created a great class of peasant proprietors in this part of England who come down generation after generation, century after century, on their own lands—twenty to thirty acres as a general rule—and give to the later history of the midland village a character quite unlike that of "unfree" villages elsewhere in the country. In these unfree villages of, say, south-western England, it is the squire who is the centre of village life and activity, together with his satellite the parson, because he owns most if not all the parish. In hundreds of midland villages we should have found no resident lord or squire, but a more or less large class of free peasants who owned a substantial part of the parish, if not most of it, between them, and who, in the early centuries at any rate, were roughly equal economically as well as socially.

These peasant proprietors, descendants for the most part of the disbanded Danish soldiers and their families of the late ninth and early tenth centuries, frequently bearing Scandinavian names long afterwards, were the ancestors of the yeomen of the fifteenth century and later, that prominent and important class of men in the Midlands, who lasted for several centuries.

And the yeomen in turn give birth to many an eminent family in Church and State. Latimer's father was a Leicestershire yeoman, Benjamin Franklin's father was a yeoman of Northamptonshire, and his ancestors had farmed their own thirty acres at Ecton since the fourteenth century at least (the very name of "franklin" would tell us if we did not know otherwise); the poet Herrick originated from one of those Scandinavian freeholders, and Swift's mother was of the same family. "My father was a yeoman" must have been the words, not untouched with pride, of many an eminent man in Elizabethan and Stuart England, and to these ranks of the learned, the great and the rich, the midland yeomen contributed their full quota.

With the Scandinavian infusion, the English mixture was virtually complete. The Normans added very little either to the blood of the ordinary English families or to the towns, villages, and hamlets of the countryside. By the eleventh century nearly every village and hamlet that appears on the map today was already in existence: the main design of the rich pattern had been drawn, and only the details needed filling in.

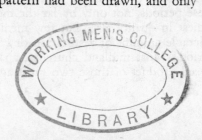

III

CHURCH AND MONASTERY

FOR two hundred years after their coming into the Midlands, the Anglo-Saxons were pagans. The heathen cemeteries of this period (450–650) have been found all over this part of England, most often whilst digging gravel for the new turnpike roads in George III's time. One of these cemeteries now lies immediately under a modern cemetery, which was laid out when the village churchyard was full with forty generations of country men and women, so that the heathen founders of the village now lie in consecrated ground whether they like it or not. The grave-diggers of today sometimes throw up fragments from this earlier level, an old rusted brooch or pin, and break through the stones that covered the sixth-century men and women.

In 653 Middle England was converted to Christianity by the marriage of its king with the daughter of the Christian king of Northumbria. Four priests immediately began the conversion of the heart of England, and for the next thirteen hundred years Christian churches were being built, beginning with Peterborough (20, 38) (Medeshamstede), Brixworth (19), and Breedon (Leicestershire) all before the seventh century was out.

Within this great stretch of time, there have been four major building periods:

    (1) the pre-Conquest period   .   . *c.* 960–1066
    (2) the early medieval   .   .   .*c.* 1150–1350
    (3) the late medieval .   .   .*c.* 1475–1535
    (4) the Victorian   .   .   .*c.* 1840–1900

The bulk of the finest work can be attributed to the second of these periods, not only by far the most prolific but in general the richest in quality also, but few medieval churches escaped a considerable amount of restoration or rebuilding in the late medieval period. Most midland churches, apart from the modern, are the mixed product of those two great ages of building. Only a small

18　Great Paxton, Huntingdonshire: mid-eleventh-century building

19　Brixworth, Northamptonshire: the finest seventh-century building
north of the Alps, *c.* 670

21 Eaton Bray, Bedfordshire: a beautiful thirteenth-century arcade

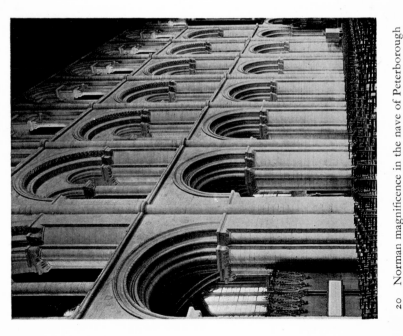

20 Norman magnificence in the nave of Peterborough Cathedral

minority are wholly in one style, but where we come across them they are almost invariably of excellent quality.

The earliest church in the Midlands was the great abbey of Medeshamstede, in the meadows of the Nene, founded originally in 654 and refounded in the tenth century as Peterborough. The first abbey was wholly destroyed by the Danes in 870 and nothing of it survives, but at Brixworth (19), in the heart of Northamptonshire, its missionary church, built c. 670, still stands much as it was then built, "perhaps the most imposing architectural memorial of the seventh century yet surviving north of the Alps" (Sir Alfred Clapham, in *Romanesque Architecture in England*). Brixworth has been described so often that I need not do so again here: the reader is referred to Sir Alfred Clapham's book as the most authoritative account of this remarkable building.

Although we know that a number of early churches or *minsters* were founded within a generation or two after 653 nothing else has survived the onslaught of the Danes in the ninth century except a finely sculptured stone frieze at Breedon-on-the-Hill (Leicestershire) which dates from the late eighth century and is now preserved inside the parish church. Presumably this frieze was taken down and hidden from the Danes as not another stone remains of the early monastery on this site, nor is there a trace left of Repton and Oundle monasteries, which perished at the same time.

Thus it is that most of the pre-Conquest building of the Midlands, the finest of which is to be found in Northamptonshire, dates from the century between 960 and 1066. In this period we have the towers of Earls Barton, Barnack, and Brigstock, and the greater part of Wittering, all in or near the rich corridor of the Nene valley and representing perhaps the finest group of Anglo-Saxon work in England.

Other notable pre-Conquest work in the Midlands is to be seen at Repton, where the chancel, crypt, and part of the nave are late tenth century in date; the nave of St. Nicholas, Leicester (late tenth or early eleventh century) and the notable church at Wing, in mid-Buckinghamshire. At Great Paxton (18), beside the Ouse in Huntingdonshire, the church is almost entirely mid-eleventh century in date. It is a monument of pre-Conquest architecture and worth going far to see: but it is more than merely an antiquary's delight, with its whitewashed interior, and its oil lamps with their characteristic white shades and faint nostalgic smell of paraffin: and the tablet on the chancel wall that commemorates the rector's son, killed in Flanders in that far-away November of 1914, "leading his men". Already he is a shadowy part of the long, receding history of the old church by the river, to which his father came as rector more than fifty years ago, and where he played as a child on the rectory lawn, in those placid years before we knew the Age of War was about to begin. It was another and a happier world than this and the tablet on the chancel wall marks the end of it.

Anglo-Saxon work may be found scattered throughout many other churches in the Midlands: in the tower arch of Market Overton (Rutland) and the tower of Clapham (Bedfordshire) and in the fine churchyard crosses of Rothley and Sproxton, both in Leicestershire, and both tenth century in date.

Of Norman architecture there is not much that is outstanding until we reach the middle of the twelfth century, the most notable exceptions being the earliest work at Peterborough (begun in 1117); Castor, not far away, which was completed and dedicated in 1125; St. Sepulchre at Northampton and St. Nicholas at Leicester; and the magnificent church of Melbourne, in Derbyshire but this side of the Trent (c.1140). Here and there one finds remote country churches, too, with impressive remains of those days, as at Lillingstone Dayrell in the quiet, unspoiled country of North Buckinghamshire, bordering upon Northamptonshire, where there is a striking chancel arch of late eleventh-century date with a contemporary nave.

Among the ordinary town and village churches, however, it is after 1160 that we find the true wealth of the Midlands. The heavy clays of the Midlands were slow to yield their full harvest and the anarchy of Stephen's reign hit these parts hard. We know from a taxation return of 1156, three years after the Civil War had ended, that nearly two-thirds of Warwickshire had been laid waste, over a half of Nottinghamshire, Derbyshire, and Leicestershire, and nearly a third of Northamptonshire. By 1162, when another return was made, most of this "waste" had disappeared from the record.

It is not surprising, then, to find that late Norman work is fairly abundant in the Midlands, and also that Transition Norman (c. 1170–1200) is common all the way from the Trent down to the Thames, though it is wholly absent from large parts of England (such as East Anglia) and very rare elsewhere. A good deal of this work must be accounted for by the reconstruction of the destroyed churches, but much, no doubt, arose from the growing prosperity and population of the last quarter of the twelfth century.

Going from north to south through the Midlands, we find, to cite only the outstanding examples, fine late Norman work at St. Mary de Castro, Leicester; Tickencote (Rutland), Wakerley (Northamptonshire), and St. Peter's, Northampton; Dunstable (Bedfordshire) and Stewkley (Buckinghamshire). Apart from these notable examples, most of the Midland counties show some late Norman work in a score or so of their village churches, though it is commoner in some parts than others. Between the Trent and the Welland it is not common, until we go eastwards towards Rutland.

22　A country interior at Shelton, Bedfordshire

23   Olney, Buckinghamshire from across the Ouse

24   Ramsey, Huntingdonshire: Norman and Perpendicular building

25 The lantern-tower of Lowick, Northamptonshire: fifteenth century

26 Higham Ferrers, Northamptonshire: Early English tower and Late
Perpendicular school

28   Exton (largely rebuilt in 1846)

27   Ketton: the thirteenth-century tower and later spire

TWO SUPERB RUTLAND CHURCHES

There we find it at Allexton (Leicestershire) within a few yards of the Rutland boundary, and at Morcott, South Luffenham, and Tixover (all in Rutland). In Northamptonshire there is a great deal of good Norman work, mostly late in the twelfth century; there are said to be some thirty or more churches where it is conspicuous. There is very little late Norman work elsewhere in the Midlands: Huntingdonshire has almost none: Bedfordshire has little apart from the monastic remains of Dunstable and Elstow; in Oxfordshire the Norman churches are small and infrequent; in Buckinghamshire there are several churches with rich Norman doorways or chancel arches, but very little else.

Similarly, too, Rutland and Northamptonshire have the best of the Transition Norman work, done in the last quarter of the twelfth century: it is commonest in these counties and in the parts of Leicestershire adjoining them. In Leicestershire we find it well developed at Theddingworth and Bringhurst in the Welland valley; at Twyford, scarcely five miles from Rutland; and at Hallaton, in the south-east of the county, not far from the Welland. In Rutland the style is found at its finest in the secular building of the castle hall at Oakham (c. 1180), but it is well developed also in the churches of Belton, Burley, Glaston, Hambleton, North Luffenham, Ryhall, Seaton, and Wing; while the west front of Ketton is superb work of the same period (c. 1190–1200) though rather a combination of late Norman and Early English—the chevron, the pointed arch, and the foliaged capital—than a transitional style proper. In Northamptonshire work of this period is very common; one finds traces of it in scores of churches. It appears at its best, perhaps, at Rothwell, in the tower of Spratton, at Hargrave (near Raunds) and in the nave of Moreton Pinkney.

Huntingdonshire has a few good examples, the best being the parish church of Ramsey (24), with a beautiful nave (c. 1180) and a groined chancel roof. Then there is the interesting church at Alwalton, not far away. Here the Norman pillars and arches have distinctive Early English mouldings and ornament, while in the south doorway the Norman chevron is used over a pointed arch. A few miles to the south, Glatton (close to the Northamptonshire border again) has a lofty nave of this period; and yet farther to the south, the remote little mid-Huntingdonshire church of Barham also dates mainly from these years. Down in Oxfordshire the style is fairly common, especially in the west of the county (which, being over the Cherwell, is outside our province); Alkerton in the north, near Banbury, is another very interesting example of the transition from Norman into Early English.

Looking at the distribution of all the best work done between c. 1160 and 1200, one cannot help noticing that it is to be found largely in the great stone belt of the central Midlands; and this is equally true of the Early English period that follows. It looks as though the stone country was growing prosperous the best part of a hundred years earlier than the clay country to the north and south. In the stone country the finest churches fall largely into the period 1160–1260; in the clay country (with few exceptions) the great age of rebuilding of churches began about 1280 and reached its peak in the second quarter of the fourteenth century.

There is not much notable Early English work on the clays between the Trent and Welland. Nottinghamshire shows almost nothing, Leicestershire very little that is characteristic of the period except where the stone belt of Northamptonshire and Rutland encroaches on the east. The Early English work of Cold Overton is within a few yards of the Rutland border, and the fine towers and broach spires of Hallaton and Great Easton (early to mid-thirteenth century) are not far from the Welland. The central tower of Melton Mowbray is another example, clearly influenced by the superb towers of Ketton and St. Mary's, Stamford, with which it is contemporary. Indeed it is possible that the three towers are all the work of the same master-builder.

The most notable churches of both Rutland and Northamptonshire are largely Early English in date. In Rutland the finest of all is Ketton (27), a noble building throughout (c. 1190–1250), though its chancel was almost entirely rebuilt by Sir Gilbert Scott a hundred years ago. The belfry stage of the tower is a masterpiece. Then there is the tower of Langham church, a handsome and spacious building altogether: as at Ketton, the broach spire was added in the next century. Ryhall church, just outside Stamford, is excellent Early English work; Great Casterton, three miles away across country, is another good building (unrestored) of the same date and of great interest. Little Casterton, half-way between the two, is mainly a thirteenth-century building but heavily over-restored. The whole of this district around Stamford abounds in interesting work of the Early English period, so much so that it is impossible to pick and choose further without laying oneself open to criticism: but the very fine church at Empingham (with beautiful work of the thirteenth, fourteenth, and fifteenth centuries) cannot fail to be mentioned. It is one of the finest buildings in a county notable for good churches.

The Early English churches of Northamptonshire have long been a pilgrimage for lovers of English church architecture, above all the northern half of the county, along both sides of the Nene. Finest of all is Warmington, a perfect text-book of the development of Early English architecture, from the nobly proportioned nave (c. 1200) to the fine wooden-groined roof (c. 1260). The south aisle

30 Titchmarsh: fifteenth century

29 Whiston: built in ironstone and limestone, c. 1535

PERPENDICULAR BUILDING IN NORTHAMPTONSHIRE

32 St. Neots, Huntingdonshire, *c.* 1480–1500

31 Liddington, Rutland: late fifteenth century

TWO FIFTEENTH-CENTURY INTERIORS

windows are beautiful grouped lancets of the first half of the century; those of the north aisle show good geometric tracery c. 1260, the date also of the clerestory. The tower and broach spire are Early English work at its most beautiful, elaborately ornamented, fine, bold and yet graceful building. The whole building, but for minor details, belongs to the Early English period. Three or four miles away are Oundle and Polebrook, both outstandingly good. The proportions and detail of Polebrook are alike excellent, above all perhaps the arcading of the north transept, the windows and other detail of the chancel, and the north porch. The furniture, too, is worth studying—screen, benches, chairs, pulpit, and medieval iron lectern.

Farther up the Nene valley are Stanwick, with its beautiful and unusual octagonal tower of the thirteenth century; Higham Ferrers (26), especially the west front of the tower (the spire was added early in the next century), and Raunds, a fine tower surmounted again by a later spire. The church is the only thing worth looking at in Raunds, which, so far as attractiveness goes, is as uncompromisingly ugly as its name. Strixton and Etton are also notable small churches of this period, though the former was disastrously rebuilt in 1874. Etton lies remote on the edge of the fens, seven miles from Peterborough, in country that is rich in both literary and antiquarian interest. This is John Clare's country, for he was born at Helpston, only a mile or two away; and much of his poetry reflects its homely charm, especially of the days before the enclosure of the heaths and the disappearance of so much of its old human and natural quality and life. As for the antiquary, he has for his sober delight the two remarkable medieval houses of Woodcroft and Northborough; the pre-Conquest work of Barnack is only four miles away and Wittering three miles beyond that; the highly interesting church of Maxey is two miles along another road; and nearly all the villages round about have excellent domestic building in stone of the seventeenth and eighteenth centuries.

The early wealth of Northamptonshire and Rutland, as reflected in their church architecture, arose in the first place from their famous quarries. The medieval builder used everything from granite to chalk, but the finest building stone came from the oolitic limestone belt, and of this the "Barnack Rag" was supreme, being of great durability. The Barnack quarries were worked in Roman times: in the seventh century they supplied the stone for Medeshamstede Abbey, and in later centuries Ely and Peterborough, Crowland, Thorney, and Ramsey, besides innumerable smaller churches round about, and numerous castles. The stone went in vast quantities up and down the rivers, as far as the Norfolk marshland, and even by sea to Rochester. So great was the demand that the quarries were exhausted by the sixteenth century, and only the broken ground round the village remains to show where all this tremendous activity once went on, at its height in the twelfth and thirteenth centuries: the rumble of the falling stone, the sawing and the shouting, the stamp of the horses and the creaking of the laden carts, on their way from quarry to waterside or through the barley-fields to some great Midland castle.

Ketton and Weldon took the place of Barnack stone. Old St. Paul's came largely out of the Weldon quarries, and Kirby Hall at a later date; and several of the Cambridge colleges out of Ketton. At Colly Weston, the lowest levels of the limestone can be split into thin layers by the action of frost, so producing the famous slates which have been used for roofing since the fourteenth century and possibly a little earlier. Like Swithland slates in Leicestershire (a true slate) Colly Westons were quarried by the Romans for their villas, but the industry lapsed with their going, and was resumed only in the late thirteenth century or the early fourteenth.

At Harleston, in the heart of Northamptonshire, were the most famous quarries of ironstone, worked for many centuries. We know that ironstone was being quarried in the twelfth century in both eastern Leicestershire and eastern Buckinghamshire; there can be little doubt that the Harleston quarries are as old as that. At Stanion, stone was being quarried in Roman times: in Edward I's time stone from here went to the repair of Rockingham Castle, and it can be found also in many local churches. But these were only the most notable quarries, and nearly every village throughout Northamptonshire and Rutland had its own little quarry at hand which supplied its own needs.

It was not only that the quarries of the Stone Belt produced stone on the spot for building fine churches cheaply, almost regardless of expense, and that where they were famous over a wide area the sale of stone and its carriage gave employment and brought prosperity. This helps to account for the early prosperity of this part of the Midlands from the middle of the twelfth century, but it is not the whole story. It seems likely that even in the purely agricultural villages of the stone country the lighter soil was more easily cleared and brought under cultivation than the heavy back-breaking clays to the north (Leicestershire) or to the south and east (Buckinghamshire and Huntingdonshire), so that the expanding fields of the stone villages reached the frontiers of the township at an earlier date, and supported a denser population in the twelfth and thirteenth centuries.

There is, of course, very good Early English work in the clay lands, as at Alconbury, Warboys, and Bury (in Huntingdonshire) or at Eaton Bray (21) (in Bedfordshire), and Chetwode (in Buckinghamshire), all outstandingly good in their own way. One cannot explain away all the exceptions by a general theory, nor would one wish to, for these sudden unexpected variations from the normal have a special appeal of their own.

The great age for rebuilding in the clay country begins in the last quarter of the thirteenth century and goes on until the Black Death brought it to a sudden end in 1349. There were, of course, hundreds of little Norman churches, many of them slightly enlarged in Early English times, in the claylands: but it is not until about 1280 that the wave of rebuilding on a larger and more costly scale reached the clay country. In Nottinghamshire it is the Decorated work which has been called "the glory of the county", and it is certainly so over most of Leicestershire. Gaddesby and Stoke Golding were wholly rebuilt between 1290 and 1340, and take a high place among the village churches of England. Loughborough and Melton Mowbray were almost wholly rebuilt on a large scale in the same years, while among the smaller churches Kegworth, Appleby Magna, Belton, and Kibworth are entirely in the Decorated style and are all good. Almost all the finest work in Leicestershire falls into these fifty years, including, besides that just mentioned, the lovely tower and spire of Market Harborough and the equally lovely chancel at Claybrook Parva.

That the period from 1250 to 1350 was one of prosperity throughout the Midland countryside, and of populous villages enjoying that "full employment" that we still strive to recover, is abundantly illustrated from the records of the country towns and villages in these times. Over and over again one finds that the village whose history one is unearthing had more people in the thirteenth century than in Elizabethan days, often many more than it has today.

I spoke just now of the fine village church at Claybrook, on the southern border of Leicestershire. We find in 1279 (when a particularly informative record was made for a wide area of the Midlands) that Claybrook Magna and Claybrook Parva, with their hamlet of Bittesby, had 70 families. At the beginning of Elizabeth's reign, when another return was made, there were 36 households in the three villages: the population had halved. At Galby, with its dependent hamlet of Frisby, there had been 39 or 40 families enumerated in the Domesday Book. In the poll-tax of 1381 about 49 households are listed, even after the repeated outbreaks of bubonic plague in the preceding generation. In the 1564 return the two places could muster only 22 families, and in 1931, after some ups and downs in the meantime, only 19. The population of Galby and Frisby today is a half what it was in the eleventh century, barely forty per cent of what it was at its greatest, in the thirteenth and fourteenth centuries. Stoney Stanton, also in Leicestershire, had 46 families in 1279, only 28 in 1564, but has grown in later centuries

by reason of its granite quarries. Wigston Magna, a large village
to the south of Leicester, with an excellent church mostly of fourteenth-century date, had getting on for 120 families in 1377 (poll-tax
return), but only 80 in 1564. One could repeat a similar story all
over the Midland counties, though most of it yet remains to be dug
out of the original records.

Not only were there more people in the villages, and abundant
evidence of thriving local industries in the thirteenth and fourteenth
centuries, but there is evidence too that manorial profits were high
during the same period. This stands out sharply if one compares
the thirteenth century with the fifteenth in the Midlands, and is
reflected faithfully again in the architecture, both church and
domestic, of the two periods. The fifteenth century was "an age of
recession, arrested economic development and declining national
income" (Professor Postan, in the *Economic History Review*, Vol. IX),
and the evidence of this decay in town and country is overwhelming
in the Midlands. The reclamation of land from the still uncleared
woodlands falls off everywhere; even in the Buckinghamshire woods
where intakes of new clearings are common in the fifteenth century,
there is nothing like the great colonising movement of the late
twelfth and thirteenth centuries. In Leicestershire, the demesne
arable on the manor of Groby had been valued at 6d. an acre in
1288; in 1445 it was down to 2d. The value of meadow fell in the
same period from 2s. an acre to 8d.; the value of the fishing in the
two great manorial ponds fell from 40s. a year to 2s., the assized
rents of the free tenants nearly halved. At Newton Harcourt, the
arable of the demesne and the village had been valued at 18s a
virgate in 1265, but in 1436 it was only 6s. As at Groby, the value
of arable land had fallen to one-third of what it had been in the
prosperous days of the second half of the thirteenth century.

There is other evidence of decay and falling profits and population, both in the towns and in the countryside. Leicester's tax quota
was cut by 20 per cent in 1445: in the villages the cut was often as high
as 30 to 40 per cent, in one place even 60 per cent. At Bottesford in
the north-eastern tip of Leicestershire, there is a fine Perpendicular
church but it is late in the style: how could it be otherwise when we
read in an inquisiton of 1440 that no fewer than twenty-two houses
in the village were worth nothing "because they are ruinous"?

An inquisition on the lands of Elizabeth de Beaumont in 1427
reveals that at both Beaumanor and Quorndon the water-mill was
"ruinous"—a sure sign of decay when the king-post of the village
economy begins to rot. At Woodhouse, on the edge of Charnwood
Forest, seventeen houses were reported ruinous and worth nothing,
"vacant for want of tenants", and the dovehouse was in ruin also;
at Quorndon twelve houses were vacant. Twenty years earlier, in

33   The Chapel at Rycote, Oxfordshire: fifteenth-century interior with
elaborate Jacobean woodwork

34   Tomb of Henry, Second Earl of
Rutland, (1563) at Bottesford, Leicestershire

35   Detail from the tomb of Robert
Kelway, (1580) at Exton, Rutland

1406, both Beaumanor and Quorndon mills had been working, but the evidence of depression in the local countryside was even then slowly accumulating. The small perquisites of the manor were steadily falling off. The bailiff records: "for ferne nothing this year, because none was sold for lack of buyers": against *flagges*, "for flagges in the pool nothing this year which used to be sold for 2s. because none were sold for the lack of buyers"; and "for croppis of willows nothing this year because none were sold".

When one comes to examine the fifteenth-century architecture of the Midland counties it corroborates the story of the records everywhere from the Trent down to the Chilterns and the Cherwell. Practically all the finest Perpendicular church-building belongs to the last quarter of the fifteenth century and the first generation of the sixteenth, when economic recovery was well on the way; and some (but very little) belongs to the closing years of the fourteenth century or the first years of the fifteenth, before the long depression had really taken root. There are very few examples of good Perpendicular church-building during the two generations between about 1420 and 1480; the exceptions (like Fotheringhay (2), mostly built 1435-60) can be explained. The same is true also of the mass of unspectacular Perpendicular rebuilding in hundreds of village and town churches all over the Midlands: hardly a church escaped some enlargement at least, or extensive repairs, in this period, but nine times out of ten it will be found to be work that is obviously late in the style.

But I was talking, before this long digression into the fifteenth century, of the great period of rebuilding in the claylands to the north, south, and east of the stone country. In Nottinghamshire, south and east of the Trent, there are many fine Decorated churches, especially so far as their chancels are concerned. Hawton, a couple of miles south of Newark-on-Trent, is especially notable: the chancel here is a masterpiece of English craftsmanship. Work by the same school of craftsmen may be seen in the chancels of Car Colston, a few miles to the south-west, and at Woodborough. Sibthorpe, between Hawton and Car Colston, is of the same quality and period. Bingham, not far from Car Colston, has a fine cruciform church with a beautiful broach spire of Decorated workmanship, and Bunny, close to the Leicestershire border and the Soar, a stately early fourteenth-century chancel. The whole of this unknown and unspoilt country between the Trent and the hills of north Leicestershire is worth exploring for its quiet landscapes, and its modestly attractive villages, many of which have churches and houses of much merit.

Over the Leicestershire border, I have spoken of the best work of this period; but apart from the outstanding work one finds many an attractive little church of these decades lying away from the main roads, like little Freeby, near Melton Mowbray, with a most attractive miniature arcade, and rustic Ragdale, in the hills between the Wreak and the Fosse Way.

In Rutland there is fine fourteenth-century building at Oakham and Langham, which have many affinities with each other. The towers of Empingham, Exton (28) and Whissendine are all beautiful, the two former being crowned with equally good spires. This is, indeed, the period of the finest spires, all up and down the limestone belt, from the magnificent work at Bloxham in North Oxfordshire up to the spires of Grantham and St. Mary's, Stamford. The spire is above all the invention of Northamptonshire builders, beginning with Wansford, Barnack, Duddington, and Kingscliffe, early in the thirteenth century, all in the extreme north of the county, and spreading and developing in the neighbouring counties by the middle of the century. The earliest spires were of the *broach* type and stumpy in appearance. Nearly every Northamptonshire church has a spire, and two in every three spires are of the broach variety, which continued to be built well into the fourteenth century. Indeed, the later ones are the best, e.g. Market Harborough (Leicestershire), Ketton (Rutland), St. Mary's, Stamford (Lincolnshire). The other type of spire, rising from the inner face of the tower wall behind a parapet, was developed in the early fourteenth century also. The beautiful soaring spires of Higham Ferrers, Oundle, and Bloxham are of this type, and are infinitely more graceful than the *broach*, good though many of these are. Leicestershire has a great number of spires of this kind, the best being perhaps those of Queniborough and Bottesford; but the broach spires of Leicestershire are often very good too, as at Hallaton, Great Easton, Harborough, and Kirby Bellars. The spires of the Midlands are one of their most characteristic sights, especially on a winter afternoon when they stand out like black needles all round the landscape, every mile or two, until a sudden flash of sunshine illuminates them, turning their limestone to a pure white in a second.

To the south of Northamptonshire spires are rare. Buckinghamshire has only two medieval spires, Olney and Hanslope, both near the Northamptonshire border, the latter mostly a rebuilding. Similarly, the most numerous and finest spires of Bedfordshire are found in the extreme north of the county, close to the Nene, along which the stone of the Northamptonshire quarries was carried. The valley of the Ouse is also thick with spires for the same reason, especially in Huntingdonshire; but to the south of the Ouse towers replace spires almost completely. The spires of Buckworth, Warboys, Old Weston, and Alconbury are all excellent, while along the road from Thrapston into Huntingdon is a whole line of excellent spired churches—Bythorn, Keyston, Brington, Spaldwick, and Ellington.

In Northamptonshire, as in Rutland, the best fourteenth-century work is to be found mainly in additions to, and enlargements of, earlier churches (e.g. the spires already mentioned, and the south porch of Woodford), but to the south we sometimes find pure examples of Decorated churches, the result of a complete rebuilding. In Bedfordshire, two of the best Decorated churches are to be found close to the Northamptonshire border—at Yelden, three or four miles east of Rushden, and Wymington, two miles south of Rushden. Wymington was rebuilt *c.* 1375 in the pure Decorated style at the expense of a wool merchant whose father had bought the manor twenty years before. It is interesting as a late survival of the Decorated style, in contrast to Shillington (Bedfordshire), rebuilt about the same time in the Perpendicular style. In Huntingdonshire, the chancel of Fen Stanton is fine Decorated work, and several churches have good work of this period though no church is outstanding.

In Buckinghamshire, Olney has a fine fourteenth-century church (23), beside the Ouse and the great water-mill. Here the chancel was rebuilt about 1330, the north and south aisles added a little later, and the western tower and spire towards the end of the century, the whole church showing good detail of the period. It is at Milton Keynes, eight miles to the south, however, that the best Decorated church in the county is to be found. The whole church was rebuilt *c.* 1330, with few traces of anything earlier except the chancel arch (late twelfth century). The fourteenth-century detail is beautiful, above all in the south doorway and porch, and in the window tracery. Clifton Reynes, just outside Olney, is also highly interesting. It contains work of every century from the twelfth to the seventeenth, but is mostly a good example of Decorated Gothic, with some remarkable fourteenth-century effigies in wood and stone.

After the opening years of the fifteenth century there is an almost complete cessation of church-building. The chancel of Adderbury, one of a group of notable churches in north Oxfordshire, was rebuilt by New College, Oxford, between 1408 and 1415, and at Fothering-hay (2) the nave and tower, crowned by its superb lantern, were added to the already existing choir in the 1430's by the royal Duke of York. The choir has since been demolished and the nave now looks too high for its length, but it remains nevertheless a splendid example of Perpendicular architecture. Fotheringhay should always be approached from the south, along the by-road from Oundle, so that the first view is the sudden vision of the whole cathedral-like building across the meadows of the tranquil river Nene, rather than the piecemeal unfolding one gets on coming from any other direction.

Most Midland churches show more or less substantial enlargement or rebuilding in the late fifteenth century or early sixteenth.
The town churches, especially, with the resurgence of prosperity
after the 1470's, show a great deal of Perpendicular Gothic at its
most beautiful. In Leicester, the tower and chancel of St. Margaret's
are noteworthy, and in the county the churches of Melton, Market
Harborough, and Loughborough were greatly enlarged. At Melton
a magnificent clerestory of forty-eight windows was inserted,
necessitating the raising of the thirteenth-century tower by another
stage: all this work was done c. 1500. About the same time the
church of Ashby-de-la-Zouch was entirely rebuilt, probably by the
wealthy earls of Huntingdon, who lived at the castle near by. Among
the village churches, Bottesford is a fine example of late Perpendicular building, with a lofty nave and excellent clerestory, and
Withcote, a remote little building in the park of Withcote Hall,
was entirely rebuilt c. 1500-10. It is a most attractive little church,
both in its proportions and its detail, with good contemporary glass,
and fitted inside like a college chapel in the early eighteenth century.

In Rutland, Liddington church (31) was completely rebuilt except
for the tower, probably in the last quarter of the fifteenth century
when John Russell, bishop of Lincoln from 1480 to 1495, rebuilt
the episcopal palace hard by. The Laudian chancel is noteworthy,
with the altar table surrounded by rails on all sides, the whole dated
1635. There is good Perpendicular work at Empingham and
Langham, and most of the Stamford churches were largely rebuilt
in this period. St. Martin's at Stamford is a fine church entirely in
the Perpendicular style (rebuilt c. 1480), and contains some magnificent tombs of the Cecils, who still live at Burghley, just outside the
town. The marble and alabaster tomb of the great Lord Burghley
(1599) is especially striking.

In Northamptonshire there is much late Perpendicular building
of great excellence. The beautiful tower and spire of Kettering
must be known to every traveller on the railway from St. Pancras.
Almost the whole church is of the same period, a notable example
of a Perpendicular town-church. Fotheringhay has already been
noticed: and at Lowick and Nassington the lantern-tower has been
copied. Lowick (25) is another beautiful church, early fifteenth
century in date and including contemporary benches and fine alabaster tombs. The Perpendicular tower of Titchmarsh (30), across
the Nene from Lowick, is one of the finest in Northamptonshire,
and is unusual in this part of England in resembling the great towers
of Somerset. But among all the Perpendicular building in Northamptonshire, perhaps even of the Midlands as a whole, the superb
little church of Whiston (29) stands out. It stands well on an
eminence above the village which clusters at its foot, on the southern

flank of the Nene valley, looking across to the more famous Earl's Barton, two miles due north; and of the two, if a choice were demanded, I would go to Whiston every time.

Whiston was completely rebuilt by the Catesbys in 1534 and is a perfect example of Perpendicular building at its latest and finest, at least so far as village churches are concerned. It is notably handsome externally where the tawny ironstone and silver-grey limestone have been combined with striking effect, and the windows are of excellent proportion. Internally, the nave is full of grace and vigour: the rich treatment of the stonework, especially in the arcade, and the proportions throughout, ought to have made Whiston an object of pilgrimage long ago. All the original benches (c. 1500) remain intact, and the beautiful original roofs also.

Moving eastwards into Huntingdonshire, the finest work of the period is to be seen in St. Neots, again late in the fifteenth century. It is mainly the work of the 1480's and 1490's, finishing with the pinnacles of the tower (1530). St. Neots has a noble fifteenth-century interior (32), with lofty nave arcades and fine clerestories, culminating in a carved roof which is now in process of being re-coloured. Elsewhere in the county the churches of Buckden, St. Ives, Wistow, and Connington have interesting Perpendicular work, all late, and similarly in Bedfordshire where all the best building in this style is late—Marston Mortaine, Cople, Willington, and Totternhoe. The Perpendicular spires of Bedfordshire are particularly good and bear comparison with those of its neighbour Northamptonshire (e.g. Sharnbrook, Harrold, Poddington, Pertenhall, and Keysoe).

In Buckinghamshire, Maids Morton, just outside Buckingham, is practically untouched late Perpendicular work of excellent design and detail, with a particularly beautiful tower. Hillesden is an equally fine and complete example of the same style with much contemporary glass and woodwork; and the chancel of North Marston is of great beauty. Edlesborough, mostly a dignified thirteenth-century church, has a wealth of Perpendicular woodwork in its roofs, rood-screen, pulpit and canopy, benches and stalls, all magnificent pieces of English craftsmanship. If one tried to enumerate religiously, however, even the outstanding examples of Midland craftsmanship in wood and stone and iron, the result would be a stultifying catalogue; and I know well enough that I have said nothing of a multitude of these works of art that are to be found from one end of the Midlands to the other, masterpieces created for the most part by local craftsmen whose names are almost invariably, though not always unknown to us. Some of these achievements, like the alabaster tombs of Bottesford (34) (Leicestershire), Exton (Rutland) (35), Great Brington and Lowick (Northamptonshire) are by known craftsmen and artists, but the greater part—the magnificently carved Perpendicular roofs, the bench-ends and stalls, and all the other woodwork, and the ironwork on doors or in railings—were done by men whose names are nowhere recorded, though we can sometimes trace their distinctive handiwork from church to church. Later, the finest works of art in our churches and houses are by men of national reputation, as the field of economic and social life widened; but in the earlier centuries, up to Tudor times anyway, the normal limit of the horizon was half a dozen miles or so, and within this radius most of the unknown craftsmen who produced such masterpieces must have lived. Not all produced masterpieces; much that was poor has perished long ago; but the general level is one of beautiful craftsmanship that is a pleasure to examine. Even where the work is in a rather homely rustic style, one recognises it with a smile of affection, like the woodwork in the little unspoilt country churches of Dean and Shelton (22) in north Bedfordshire, with their uneven, stone-slabbed floors, their bench-ends leaning first one way and then the other with the irregularity of long use, and the sunlight on the old oak of the benches, which shine with a patina given by country hands and seats for the last fifteen generations. For all the talk of dates and periods and styles, what impresses one most after all in these multitudes of village and small-town churches is the evidence everywhere of careful, loving workmanship, however countrified it may be, the attention to detail, the lifetime of knowledge that lay behind all this craftsmanship in wood and stone and iron, the great reservoir of skill and dignity which every village then possessed as a matter of course. One can still feel a little of the satisfaction those old men must have felt when they had finished the new roof for the nave, or the new benches or the screen, and, looking at it, saw that it was good. And in a way one feels that it is as well their names are not known to us and never will be known, for they will never be classified and catalogued, dated and annotated in text-books, and the life sucked out of their work. As it is, nothing stands between their work and us.

By the time the Reformation came church-building was nearly finished. Every village had its church, every hamlet of any size had its little chapel served once, twice, or three times a week from the mother church. And as so many villages had fewer people in the sixteenth century than in the thirteenth, there was even less incentive to rebuild and enlarge. Most of the rebuilding done in the villages in the fifty years or so after 1475 must have been necessitated by the disrepair and decay of the preceding two generations of depression, except perhaps in special cases like the Catesbys' desire to rebuild the village church of Whiston completely—and even this may have been occasioned by the sad state the old church had got into. In the towns, on the other hand, the revival of merchants' trading profits did produce a genuine desire to build larger and finer fabrics, as at St. Neots and Melton Mowbray, but this impulse might well have waned during the sixteenth century even had there been no Reformation; for men were becoming more worldly minded and eager to enjoy the fruits of this world as the opportunities for material gain opened out in more and more enchanting vistas.

There is very little church-building in the Midlands after 1535, until we come to the Gothic Revival churches of the nineteenth century, made necessary by the growth of the boot and shoe trades and the hosiery villages. But because churches in the Elizabethan and Stuart period are so rare, they become all the more interesting, and some of them are delightful little buildings unsurpassed for charm by anything earlier. In Bedfordshire the little church of Holcot, on the borders of Buckinghamshire, was entirely rebuilt by the lord of the manor in Elizabethan times. It is full of seventeenth-century, made necessary by the growth of the boot and shoe trades were responsible for building the church. Not far away, on the Buckinghamshire side, is the excellent little late seventeenth-century church of Willen, built of red and black bricks with limestone dressings, about 1680. All the detail, except the modern apse, is of this period. It is said to be from designs by Wren, and this may be so.

A perfect day's walking would begin at Newport Pagnell, on to Willen and thence to Milton Keynes; from here along quiet lanes over the Bedfordshire border to little Holcot, where there is no village;[1] and thence southwards towards the greensand hills, up to Aspley Heath, more than five hundred feet up (a great height in this part of the country) with wide views over the claylands, and down again through delightful Bow Brickhill with its many seventeenth-century houses, back to Fenny Stratford.

Three miles along another road from Newport Pagnell, which is a good centre for visiting much unspoilt country and many interesting villages and churches, lies the beautiful church of Gayhurst (37), rebuilt in the classical style in 1728. Gayhurst is sometimes said to be by Wren; it is certainly of the Wren school. It is a perfect early eighteenth-century interior (36), with a fine monument to Sir Nathan Wright and his son, and all the furnishings of the period. The *Little Guide* to Buckinghamshire, one reads with a sense of shock, till recently said briefly of Gayhurst: "the church is a wretched building, showing much 18th-century rubbish, and was built in 1728". When one reads this judgment, written just over forty years ago and re-printed as recently as 1918, one hesitates to condemn even mid-Victorian stained glass, executed in the 1860's and 1870's, lest a

---

[1] Holcot, I am told, is now disused and shamefully neglected, as also is Faxton in the heart of Northamptonshire, another abandoned village site.

coming generation should discover beauty in it to which we are quite insensitive (and indeed some early Victorian stained glass is very pleasing and is already being "collected"). Just as Regency architecture and furniture were despised not so long ago, and are now recognised at their true worth, so taste is moving on in time towards the early Victorian houses and furniture. The worst Gothic Revival churches of the Midland towns may yet be singled out for praise: but I must confess the imagination falters at this.

At the northern end of the Midlands, almost on the very banks of the Trent, stands Foremark church, rebuilt in 1662 in what used to be called a "debased" Gothic, an interesting little building that is well worth visiting after leaving Melbourne, which is four miles to the east, and before going on into Repton. Five miles to the south-east of Foremark, up in the hills and just over the Leicestershire border, is Staunton Harold church (52), entirely rebuilt in the Cromwellian period of all times, by Sir Robert Shirley "whose singular praise it is", we are told on the inscription over the door, "to have done the best things in the worst of times". This church, too, is in a seventeenth-century version of Gothic; the interior is a perfect, unspoilt Cromwellian period-piece.

Elsewhere in Leicestershire, Great Dalby was largely rebuilt about 1661, after the old spire had fallen into the nave on the first night of the year 1658. The event is recorded thus in the parish register, by a later incumbent who had the details from an old man in the village:

> "The steeple, being an high spire, fell upon the body of the church, on the 2d day of January 1658, and brought to the ground the North aile and the middle aile, leaving only standing part of the chancel and the South aile. It was very large and beautiful, the roof of the high leads counted the best carved work in all Leicestershire. On the south part of the wall of the high leads were the arms of *England* and *Mowbray*. It fell on the very morning of the Lord's day, about one o'clock. It gave us warning all that night before, by stones falling down on the bells. I was told, in the year above (1771) by a venerable old gentleman, a bachelor, whom I buried soon after at the age of 88, that, by tradition from father to son, he heard, they had rung the old year out, and new in, much and long, by uncommon exertions; and that it was a miraculous and providential escape, the steeple did not fall on the heads of the ringers, or, by a protraction of a small portion of time, on the congregation assembled for Divine Worship."

The damage was assessed at £1660, for the making good of which the parish sent out an appeal which had unfortunate results. For "it was traditionally stated on the spot, that the parish, upon this great loss, sent out two persons of good address, with a petition, well attested, containing the particulars; who not only made their

37   The exterior from the south west

36   The chancel and reredos

GAYHURST, BUCKINGHAMSHIRE, 1728

38   Peterborough Cathedral: formerly the Abbey Church. The Norman
nave and south transept and Decorated central tower

application in the vicinity, but a great part of the kingdom; and thus obtained a large sum of money towards rebuilding the edifice; but, having contracted a dissipated life by their perambulation, and not frequently called upon to give an account of their commission, they ran away with the whole sum". The necessary money was collected once more, locally and in churches all over the country by means of a brief, and in due course the building as we see it today was completed, a not unattractive building with large square-headed windows of plain glass that let in plenty of light.

Another little seventeenth-century church is at Owthorpe, now a mere hamlet in the broad clay vale that lies between the Trent and the Belvoir escarpment of north Leicestershire. Owthorpe was the home of the parliamentarian Colonel Hutchinson, the defender of Nottingham Castle in the Civil War, who retired to his quiet home after the storms of war had blown themselves out, and rebuilt his house and the church in the 1650's.

In Northamptonshire, the church of All Saints, Northampton, was rebuilt in the classical style after the great fire of 1675 which devastated a large part of the town, but it is in Huntingdonshire that we find the two most notable seventeenth-century churches in the Midlands—Little Gidding and Leighton Bromswold, both associated with George Herbert and the Ferrars.

Little Gidding stands on rising land between the Nene and the Ouse valleys, on the borders of Northamptonshire and Huntingdonshire, and just inside the latter county. It is now a place of pilgrimage for the Anglican Church, as the home of the religious community founded here in Charles I's time by Nicholas Ferrar, a young London merchant. About forty of the family and their relatives came to this remote spot in 1625 to escape one of London's recurrent plagues, and here they found the village all gone, the manor-house in ruins, and the church used for keeping hay and pigs. Here the little community toiled to rebuild the church and manor-house, and here they were visited twice by the sympathetic King Charles. Nicholas Ferrar died in 1637, only forty-four years old; he did not live to see his house and church wrecked again by Puritan soldiers and his community broken up. Today, the manor-house he built is gone without a trace, and of his original church probably only the chancel remains. The remainder was rebuilt in 1714, in a good time for building, and the interior is wholly of this quiet age. Nicholas Ferrar lies in the table tomb as one approaches the west door of the church, inside which there are brasses to his family, including one to Susanna, his only daughter, who was blessed with eight sons and eight daughters and who lived nevertheless to be seventy-six.

Leighton Bromswold lies between four and five miles across

country from Little Gidding, and John Ferrar (brother of Nicholas) used to ride over three times a week from Little Gidding to see to the building operations, over these windy, open, clay ridges with such great far-seeing views though less than two hundred feet above the sea. Leighton Bromswold was rebuilt between 1626, when George Herbert became patron and lay rector of the living, and 1634, which is the date on the tower. Both externally and internally the church is practically as it was when finished, a perfect Carolean interior, with a reading-pew and pulpit on either side of the chancel-arch, and all the other furniture of the time.

Of eighteenth-century church-building, there is Gayhurst already mentioned, and Melchbourn and Segenhoe in Bedfordshire, both largely or partly rebuilt in the latter part of the century. I do not know of any noteworthy eighteenth-century churches in North-amptonshire, but I feel sure there must be one or two hidden away in remote corners, despised and rejected by guide-books and there-fore only to be come upon by blind chance. Even the Royal Commission on Historical Monuments until recently drew the line at 1714, and at this rate it will be a long time before the excellent and seemly architecture of the early nineteenth century is discovered and recorded. In Rutland there is Teigh church, rebuilt in 1782 except for the tower, and arranged internally like a college chapel, with stalls facing each other across the nave, as was so often done in this period. Normanton has a tower and portico, built in 1826, copied from the tower of St. John's, Westminster; but the body of the church, in the same style, was added in 1911.

In Leicestershire there is good eighteenth-century building at King's Norton (1770), Stapleford (1783), Galby (1741), Snarestone (1733), and Wistow—the last with some very fine ironwork of early eighteenth-century date. King's Norton is the best of these later churches; it is excellent all the way from its wrought-iron gates onwards. Over the border, in Nottinghamshire, there are Kinoulton (1793), and Rempstone (1771), not far from each other at the foot of the north Leicestershire wolds.

During the eighteenth century, and the early nineteenth, many pleasant Nonconformist chapels were built, plain and seemly build-ings, of which the Great Meeting (1708), in a now unfashionable part of old Leicester, is a very good example. After 1840 both church and chapel architecture changed spectacularly for the worse. Generally speaking, the chapels are incomparably worse than the churches, and invariably worse effects could be obtained in Midland brick than in any kind of stone, so that some of the most dreadful architecture in the whole of England may be seen in the industrial towns of the Midlands. There is a good deal of it, too, for the industrial revolution came late in the Midland industries, and their greatest growth took place after the middle of the nineteenth century, just when architectural taste was at its lowest. The growing towns needed more churches and chapels and schools, and in the 1860's and 1870's these were being provided in all the towns and industrial villages of Leicestershire and Northamptonshire. Even the purely rural areas in Rutland did not wholly escape the mid-Victorian chapel and school, but since many of these are necessarily built of the local stone that lay almost underfoot they do not strike the eye like the brickwork of the clay belts: they are often of excellent workmanship and, though dull in design, inoffensive.

Some of the Gothic Revival churches, especially those built towards the end of the century when architecture was becoming more restrained again, are not without merit. Early in the present century there is the very notable church of St. Mary's, Wellingborough, built largely of rich local ironstone, and still in process of being gorgeously furnished and coloured internally. Certainly it is a place to be visited if one is within twenty miles of Wellingborough at any time.

But now we must turn back in time to the monastic houses of the Midlands, of which very little, it must be confessed, remains today. Nearly everything has perished. What remains today makes one regret the splendour that has gone: Peterborough Cathedral (once the abbey church) and Dunstable church (once the nave of the great priory church) are all that is left substantially, with lesser traces at Canons Ashby (Northamptonshire), Owston and Ulverscroft (Leicestershire), Elstow (Bedfordshire), and Ramsey (Huntingdonshire). One wonders, looking at the magnificent nave and west front of Peterborough, what the great Norman abbey churches of Eynsham and Leicester were like in their splendid days: "shaken again and again", as Rilke says in one of his letters, "by the chanting and the onslaughts of the organ, by the cannonades, the tempests of song every Sunday, the hurricanes of the great festival days". And now most of them are covered with the green grass of the midland pastures—Pipewell and Sulby, Croxton and Medmenham —or buried deep in the heart of great houses that were built on their levelled foundations by the first spoliators, as at Woburn (Bedfordshire) and Garendon (Leicestershire).

The oldest and greatest of them all, the Benedictine Abbey of Peterborough, was founded as Medeshamstede about the year 654, destroyed by the Danes in 870, and refounded a hundred years later (between 966 and 970). The site of the tenth-century church is known, but the glory of Peterborough is the nave of the abbey church begun in 1117 and completed about 1220. It shows the whole range of Norman architecture from beginning to end, finishing with that magnificent Early English screen across the west front

(1200–20). But it is quite impossible to describe Peterborough in a few lines, and as it has been done so often before, I leave the task in those more competent hands, only remarking that the building has come down to us intact because it was one of the few great abbeys to be converted into a cathedral by Henry VIII, who even made its last abbot the first bishop of the new diocese: and it has also come through the last few years of bombardment (1939–45) untouched.

At the other end of the Midlands, Dunstable church (39, 40), the best in Bedfordshire, represents the Norman nave of the splendid Augustinian priory church, with a fine west front also; and at Canons Ashby (Northamptonshire) there are extensive remains of the former Augustinian priory in the west front and nave of the present parish church. Of the great Benedictine Abbey of Ramsey (founded 969) little survives except the gatehouse; of the Cistercian abbeys of the Midlands nothing is left except fragments at Warden (Bedfordshire) and old walls in the basements of Woburn (Bedfordshire) and Garendon (Leicestershire). Among the Augustinian houses, the parish church of Owston, remote in the wooded hills of East Leicestershire, was once part of the abbey church, Breedon church (Leicestershire) represents the choir of Breedon priory, and the extensive ruins of Ulverscroft priory (Leicestershire) lie in the secluded depths of Charnwood Forest. On the other side of the Forest are the ruins of the nunnery of Gracedieu, mingled with those of the Beaumonts' Tudor mansion, where Francis Beaumont was born in 1586; and down in Bedfordshire the church of Elstow marks the remains of the church of the old Benedictine nunnery.

Nearly all the monastic houses of the Midlands have perished as though they had never been, but three hundred years after their suppression, in the year 1835, there arose once more in the heart of Charnwood Forest the first monastery to be established in England since the Reformation: the Benedictine Abbey of Mount St. Bernard. It was at first only a cottage in a lonely meadow, in the depths of the Forest that had sheltered Gracedieu, Ulverscroft, and Charley in their time, inhabited only by two presbyters and four lay brothers, but within ten years a large monastery had been built and there is now a flourishing community.

39 The Norman Arcade, formerly the Priory Church

40 Norman West Door

DUNSTABLE, BEDFORDSHIRE

41 Bushmead Priory, Bedfordshire. The Perpendicular Refectory

42 Cossington Rectory, Leicestershire: Medieval and Elizabethan Work

IV

THE COUNTRY HOUSE

THE Midlands are famous for their castles and country-houses, Northamptonshire above all. Among the castles, Belvoir and Rockingham (5) still look like great strongholds; Kimbolton is now only a castle in name; Barnwell is in ruins, and Ampthill is gone. Among the country-houses, there are Burghley, Milton, Drayton (53), and Apethorpe (54), all in Northamptonshire, and all of princely size; and in the same county Althorp, Canons Ashby, Rushton, Deene (48), Boughton, Overstone, Fawsley, Castle Ashby (55), and Lilford (50) are all great houses. In Leicestershire are Stapleford, Quenby (46), Nevill Holt, Bosworth, Launde, Gopsall; in Rutland, Normanton, Exton (58), and Burley-on-the-Hill; in Huntingdonshire, Kimbolton (49), Hinchingbrooke, and Connington; in Bedfordshire, Woburn and Ampthill; in Buckinghamshire north of the Chilterns, Gayhurst and palatial Stowe. But besides all these great houses, lesser country-houses of beauty and distinction lie thickly scattered over the landscape, above all in or near the stone belt: Northamptonshire has scores of such beautiful manor-houses like Dingley and Cotterstock, and there are many both to the north and south of the stone country, some of them houses of great age, going back in parts to the thirteenth and fourteenth centuries.

Then there are all the great houses that have vanished or now lie in ruins; Bradgate (47), Gracedieu, Ashby (43), and Kirby Muxloe in Leicestershire; the palace of Holdenby in Northamptonshire, and Lyveden and Wothorpe in the same county; Houghton in Bedfordshire, built for the Countess of Pembroke by Inigo Jones, and magnificent Rycote (45), near Thame, built for Lord Williams in Henry VIII's time and now clean gone except for the chapel (33). The two palaces of the Bishops of Lincoln, whose diocese once stretched south to the Thames, are falling into ruin also, one at Buckden, not far from Huntingdon, and the other at Liddington in Rutland, beside the old main road from Lincoln southwards.

These country-houses and palaces of the Midlands are the result in the main of two great building periods, the first beginning with economic recovery in the 1480's and reaching its climax in Elizabethan times, though its impetus is still pronounced in the following reign which saw the creation of several lovely houses like Quenby (Leicestershire) and Connington (Huntingdonshire). The second period of large-scale building may be said to begin in the 1680's and to reach its climax with the territorial ascendancy of the nobility in Georgian times. Often the second period built on and around the work of the first, to produce the splendour and magnificence of the eighteenth-century palace. Few houses are indeed untouched work of one style; most of the large houses are a blend of sixteenth-, seventeenth- and eighteenth-century styles: plain Tudor, Renaissance beauty of detail, classical grandeur, in one house. The architectural history of that superb house of Drayton, or of lovely Apethorpe

"mourned about with troops of doves"

is a complicated story.

Before the closing years of the fifteenth century, the country-house as we know it could have no place. Wealthy men built castles for their protection, and the less wealthy built themselves in on an island site within a moat. The gently undulating clays of the Midlands, from Nottinghamshire down to the Chilterns, with their network of little streams, were ideal country for such moated homesteads and several hundred of these sites, now for the most part deserted and their moats dry, can be found today. Even in Northamptonshire there are more than thirty such moated homestead sites, of which the best is Woodcroft Castle, in lonely country though only five miles from the busy railway network of Peterborough. Woodcroft was built c. 1280 on a quadrangular plan within its moat, with a frontage of a hundred feet and a tower at either end. Within the four massive enclosing sides lay an inner courtyard (about 50 feet by 40 feet) and the domestic quarters occupied the back wing of the site, facing the gatehouse across the courtyard. Much of the original structure of Woodcroft still stands today, with some later medieval additions, and is occupied as a farmhouse.

Another notable moated manor-house which survives today, largely in its original form, is that at Hemingford Grey, near the Ouse in Huntingdonshire, a most interesting example of twelfth-century domestic architecture (c. 1160). Appleby Magna (Leicestershire) still retains its moat and late fifteenth-century gatehouse, but the dwelling-house behind is a Tudor successor of the medieval house, which had been the home of the ancient Appleby family from the early twelfth century until they fell upon evil times in Tudor days. Although, however, the original house has gone, we

43   Ashby de la Zouch Castle, Leicestershire, 1476–80
(From the engraving by Thomas Allom, 1841)

44   Ashby St. Ledger, Manor House, Northamptonshire: late sixteenth
century

The Stables

RICOTT

45 Rycote, Oxfordshire, now almost entirely demolished

(From an engraving by Henry Winstanley, c. 1690)

know from an inventory of the personal estate of Edmund de
Appleby, made in 1375, pretty much what it looked like, and how
it was furnished. Not many inventories come down to us from this
early date, giving us such a detailed picture of a medieval squire's
house and mode of living. Like the majority of fourteenth-century
squires, Edmund de Appleby held his modest estate by knight
service and could be called upon to fight overseas for the king, but
at home he was a farmer, letting out a good bit of his ancestral
lands and keeping the rest in hand for the maintenance of his own
household. The inventory reveals just such a combination of fighter
and farmer: the armour of his younger days (he had fought at Crécy,
where he had taken prisoner Robert de Mailarte, a nobleman of
France), now lying in the chamber or solar; and the stables and the
barns outside, with their horses, oxen, ploughs, carts, and other
farm-gear, and the cattle and sheep. The old house contained the
usual hall and chamber, kitchen and larder, pantry and buttery, and
a private chapel. The stables, barns, and byres completed the
buildings on the site.

The hall was very barely furnished—tables, forms, hangings, and
basins and ewers. The only item of interest is the "chymene",
evidently the latest invention at Appleby, and regarded as a piece
of movable property and not as part of the structure of the house;
just as, I believe, baths were regarded within living memory. The
chamber, or private room of the family, was most richly furnished,
with many beds of brilliant colour—ruby, blue, black, silver, white
—sumptuous hangings, cushions, blankets, and other bedding, and
basins and so forth for washing. The pantry and buttery contained
a fine collection of plate—bowls of silver and silver-gilt—tablecloths and other linen, candlesticks, tubs, bottles and barrels, ending
with "vi pottes de lether", valued at 6s. 8d. The kitchen and other
domestic offices contained much what we should expect, and outside
was the lord's stable for his grey horse, which was worth 100
shillings and three other horses, worth another hundred shillings,
altogether. The other stable held five cart-horses (worth two marks
each) and two "iron-bound" carts with gear, priced at three pounds.
Lastly, there is the farm-gear and implements, and the live-stock;
and the whole inventory is summed at £260 7s. 10d., roughly
£10,000 in modern (1939) values.

The Applebys continued at Appleby until the beginning of
Elizabeth's reign, when they sold out. George Appleby was slain
at Musselburgh field in 1547, and his widow, who married
again, was burnt at the stake just ten years later. Their son
George sold the ancestral manor in 1560 and so ended the long
association of his family with the place. From the style of the
architecture, the present house was built by the new purchaser c.

1560: it is one of the very few true "black and white" houses left in Leicestershire.

Most of these moated sites are now bare of any building, and where a building still stands it is generally later in date than the original house on the site. At Donington-le-Heath, in the Leicestershire coalfield, is the oldest inhabited house in the county, going back to the late thirteenth century. It is built of rubble masonry, of tough Charnwood stone with the soft local sandstone for dressing, buttressed like a medieval church at its corners, with its original hall-doorway clearly visible on the first floor and now mutilated to form a bedroom window. Originally it may have been like the better-preserved Markenfield Hall, in Yorkshire, where the hall, chamber, and chapel are on the first floor and are reached by an external stairway, the kitchen and cellars lying below, at ground level. The moat at Markenfield still remains, but at Donington all traces of the original defences have vanished.

Potters Marston is another well-preserved site, in the clay lowlands of the Soar valley. Much of its moat remains, and on the extensive island a Hall which is largely medieval in date, with Jacobean extensions: there is a medieval dovecote also, and a little medieval chapel of no architectural interest. In the cornfield to the east of the chapel the war-time plough struck the lost township, which disappeared under the sheep-pastures about 1500, and the pottery-kilns that gave the place its distinctive name in Henry III's day.

Down in Buckinghamshire there are a great number of these moated homesteads, though few retain their original buildings. The best is perhaps Doddershall, in the vale of Aylesbury near Quainton, a good example of early sixteenth-century domestic architecture, especially noteworthy for its hall and staircases, with a south-west wing added late in the seventeenth century. Considerable traces of the original moat remain at Doddershall, but Denham Lodge, close by, is perhaps better preserved, though its buildings are a century later in date. Here one finds, as at Appleby Magna in Leicestershire, a farmhouse and gatehouse on the island, and a fishpond near the moat.

Church Farm at Edlesborough, with a very fine timber-framed barn (mid-16th cent.) is another moated site, and so are Moat Farm at North Crawley (early 16th cent.) and Marsworth Great Farm. The best preserved medieval manor-house in Buckinghamshire—Creslow—does not seem to have been moated. It is still largely a fourteenth-century building (c. 1330), retaining most of its original hall and the whole of its solar wing.

Most of these moated manor-houses came into existence in the thirteenth and fourteenth centuries, some in the fifteenth (though not many), and probably none after Henry VII's time. They were essentially the homes of the medieval squires, who were, rather than the great feudal baronage, the most numerous and typical land-owners in the Midland counties. Greater men lived in castles, like Belvoir (Leicestershire) or Barnwell (Northamptonshire), but most of the larger castles (like Rockingham and Fotheringhay) were royal. Ashby de la Zouch Castle (43) and Kirby Muxloe Castle, both out-standing examples of medieval domestic architecture in unknown Leicestershire, are not true castles. They were built late in the fifteenth century by one of the last of the great lawless barons, William first Lord Hastings, a man of great wealth and powerful enemies, who kept a private army. He built himself at Ashby a remarkable self-contained fortress-house (1476–80) which, though it was slighted by order of Parliament in 1648, still stands boldly to a height of ninety feet, a monument of the anarchic times in which it was built.

Kirby Castle, a few miles away, was built on an already existing moated site, round a little fourteenth-century manor-house, and remains one of the most striking examples of medieval brickwork in England. It was built between 1480 and 1484, as we know from the complete building accounts that have survived and which were printed rather more than thirty years ago, with a learned intro-duction by Professor Hamilton Thompson. These accounts make fascinating reading and I wish it were possible to quote from them at length: but what stands out particularly in them is the fact that all the materials that went to the making of this great house were the product of the immediate neighbourhood: the 1,342,500 bricks used altogether in the building were made on the spot from local clay, the dressed stone came mostly from sandstone quarries about fourteen miles away, near Lord Hasting's other stronghold of Ashby, the rough stone required for the footings came from Charn-wood, the timber from parks round about, the lime from the ancient lime-pits of Barrow-on-Soar, started in the fourteenth century and working vigorously today. The great man's house, as much as the labourer's cottage and the farmer's barn, came out of the ground it stood on or at most within a few miles' radius of it: the architecture of the Midlands expressed the essence of that old, rural, self-sufficient civilisation. Barnwell Castle came out of the Barnwell limestone quarry in Henry III's time (c. 1266), Harlestone church (entirely rebuilt 1320–2) out of the Harlestone ironstone pits, the barns of Naseby from the great curved oaks that grew on those windy heights;[1] and so it was all over the Midlands, and indeed all over England in those days of sane economy.

---

[1] The parson of Naseby, writing in 1792, says too that nearly all the houses were built of "a kind of kealy earth" dug near the village "excellent in its kind, and the best calculated for building I ever saw; walls built with this exceedingly firm and strong. . . ." Some were more than two hundred years old even then.

With the establishment of a strong central government under Henry VII and the extinction or suppression of the feudal baronage of the fifteenth century, the true country-house makes its appearance. Lord Hastings's two fortified houses of Ashby and Kirby are the last expression of the old disorder; within a very few years (certainly by 1490) Thomas Grey, marquis of Dorset, had begun to build his lordly country-house in its deer-park with no thought of defence against sudden attack, at Bradgate (47) on the edge of Charnwood, almost within sight of Kirby. Like Kirby, Bradgate was built of bricks made on the site, with dressed stone at the quoins and in the doorways and window-openings. It was occupied by the Greys until about 1740, then abandoned by them for another seat in Staffordshire, and since then it has decayed into ruins. Much of it has been deliberately pulled down. Where the brickwork has not been so treated the bricks and mortar are still hard and strong after 450 years. The beautiful deer-park, together with the ruins of the old house, home of Lady Jane Grey, are now the property of the city of Leicester, some six miles away, whose citizens "go out to Bradgate" on summer evenings and at week-ends in great numbers, yet without spoiling it in any way.

Thus began the great age of country-house building. Economic recovery, after the long depression of the fifteenth century, had set in by the 1470's: trade revived, and in the countryside landlords' rents and manorial profits recovered their old level, and substantially more where the new fashion for converting arable into profitable sheep-pastures was at work. This movement, largely the work of the greater landlords (including the monastic houses, who were well to the fore), had begun in the middle of the fifteenth century and already a considerable number of villages and hamlets had been depopulated in the Midlands before the government took legislative action. But no legislation could stop this process: at best it could only slow it up; and by the end of Elizabeth's reign about fifty villages and hamlets had gone in Leicestershire alone; a great number had been under grass for a hundred years by then. Warwickshire, Northamptonshire, and Rutland told the same story.

John Spencer, a country gentleman no more conspicuous than most of his time, laid the foundations in these years of the wealth that built Althorp and furnished it with its magnificent library and picture gallery, and maintained a peerage that has ever since been a great and historic name in Northamptonshire: all out of sheep and wool. It was one of his descendants who made that devastating retort in a House of Lords debate when taunted as to his origin: "My Lord," said the Earl of Arundel, "when these things were doing, your ancestors were keeping sheep." "When my ancestors were keeping sheep," replied the first Baron Spencer of Worm-

46 Quenby Hall (1620–30): the finest Jacobean house in Leicestershire

47 Bradgate House, Leicestershire, about 1724: now a ruin
(From an engraving by H. Hulsbergh, c. 1724)

leighton, "your ancestors were plotting treason," a shot that went home.

The pictures at Althorp are notable even in the Midlands, which contain the superb collections of Belvoir, Burghley, and Woburn, among others, but the two great libraries which were accumulated there have gone elsewhere. The first, collected by the Spencer who was third earl of Sunderland, went to Blenheim with his son, who inherited that palace from his aunt and became the third duke of Marlborough. The junior branch of the Spencers remained at Althorp and acquired the title of Earl Spencer and Viscount Althorp in 1763; and it was the second Earl Spencer who gathered together an even more magnificent library which was particularly rich in early printed books. This library was bought in 1892 by Mrs. John Rylands and now forms the John Rylands Library at Manchester.

The first John Spencer, the flock-master of Henry VII's and Henry VIII's days, began the building of the present Althorp; everywhere over the Midlands the rising gentry were doing likewise. Many, if not most, of the greater Midland country-houses contain a block of early sixteenth-century building which later and wealthier owners have extended or completely encased, as at Hinchingbrooke, Burghley, Apethorpe, Kimbolton, Stapleford, and Milton, to name only the most notable. Sometimes an entirely new building was begun by a wealthy owner, like Bradgate in Leicestershire or Kirby in Northamptonshire. Building continued all through the sixteenth century, reaching a climax with the grandiose rivalry of Elizabethan statesmen and officials: Hatton building at Holdenby, Cecil at Burghley, Tresham at Rushton and Lyveden. The century up to the outbreak of the civil wars was pre-eminently that of the country gentry, who advanced everywhere at the expense of the old nobility and the Crown: it was said in 1628 that the House of Commons could buy the House of Lords three times over. The palaces of the nobility were often built by running heavily in debt to the City. When war came in 1642 it was reckoned that the royalist adherents owed the City some £2,000,000 for one reason and another, though the debtors included a great number of needy gentry as well as the "splendid spendthrifts" cited by Professor Tawney.[1] The extravagant builders of Elizabeth's time left their sons and grandsons embarrassed for money, and the lawyers and City merchants often reaped the benefit. A succession of daughters in the family, too, was a disaster of the first magnitude, for their dowries beggared the estate. At Knaptoft, in deepest Leicestershire, we see all these social changes happening clearly, from the golden beginning in sheep-pastures to the end in royalist defeat. The Turpins had acquired

[1] In a highly interesting article on "The Rise of the Gentry" 1558–1640, *Economic History Review*, vol. XI, No. 1.

the manor of Knaptoft by marriage in 1466: by the end of the century
the first generation had turned it all to sheep-pastures, the village
was gone and a new Hall rising as the visible sign of the change of
fortune. The old moated house down by the stream was abandoned
to damp and cold, and a new house built at the top of the field,
beside the church, out of the profits of the sheep-pastures. The
Turpins flourished: a knighthood came their way and their flocks
multiplied. The new Hall itself was substantially enlarged by Sir
William towards the end of Elizabeth's reign, not a palace, indeed,
but a house that was typical of those put up by the richer squires
of the time. But there were debts: money borrowed from the City
on mortgage: and then five daughters in a row meant a further
mortgage of that handsome property to Grace, Lady Manners,
member of the wealthiest landed family in all these parts, ever on the
look-out for profitable investments. Richard Turpin fell behind in
his interest payments, was on the king's side when war came and
was heavily fined by Parliament. In 1648 Lady Manners foreclosed
on the mortgage and the rich manor of Knaptoft was swallowed
up in the growing estate of the earls of Rutland, who dwelt at
the other end of the county, at Belvoir. And so Sir William's
new Hall, too, began to fall into ruin within a generation or two,
even as the village homes had tumbled down more rapidly five or
six generations earlier. Knaptoft was now owned by a great absentee
landlord and not by a resident squire, and the change was sympto-
matic of what was beginning to happen all over England. For just
as the gentry had risen, a hundred years earlier, on the ruins of the
feudal nobility and on the spoils of the monasteries, so, after 1660,
they in their turn yielded to the peerage and lost ground to them.

For the next two hundred years we see the steady accumulation of
lands by a territorial aristocracy far above the squirarchy in social
status and income, and their houses expanded accordingly. The
squire continued to live in the handsome house of his Elizabethan
or Jacobean ancestors—such as Quenby (46) and Ragdale, Dingley,
Rushton, and Connington—but the aristocracy, sometimes themselves old squires who had moved up, rebuilt on a splendid scale.
Woburn was rebuilt by the fourth duke of Bedford in the middle of
the eighteenth century; the Verneys added grandly to Claydon (56,59)
at the same time, in keeping with their new peerage; Burley-on-the-
Hill was built by Daniel Finch, Earl of Winchelsea and Nottingham,
in the closing years of the seventeenth century; Nevill Holt and
Stapleford blossomed forth in great new wings; Kimbolton (49),
begun by Sir Robert Wingfield about 1525, was magnificently
enlarged by Vanbrugh early in the eighteenth century; Stowe was
spreading its classical grandeur in Buckinghamshire; Althorp
expanded about 1688, Apethorpe (54) had been growing in every

48   Deene Hall, Northamptonshire: mid-sixteenth and early seventeenth
century

49   Kimbolton Castle, Huntingdonshire. The Courtyard from the
North-West: late seventeenth century

"Country Life" Photograph

50   Lilford Hall, Northamptonshire, 1635

51   Kirby Hall, Northamptonshire: north side of the courtyard.   John
Thorpe's work below (1570-5) and Inigo Jones's work above (1638-40)

century from the sixteenth; Milton acquired a great new garden front. Between 1680 and 1800 most of the great country-houses were still further enlarged by their noble owners, whose estates and parks were growing at the same time.

The spreading parks of the Midlands were being laid out or replanned, and planted with timber. Woburn, especially, has a long tradition of forestry. The Park, twelve or thirteen miles around, is thickly timbered with oak, chestnut, beech, and elm, the oldest planted in the early seventeenth century. A fine avenue of elms was planted in the time of George II, and on the birth of a daughter in 1743 the then Duke of Bedford planted the wood known as the "Evergreens", of Scots pine, larch, and spruce. This tradition is well maintained today: since 1900 more than six million trees have been planted at Woburn. The felling of 1914–18 cleared more than six hundred acres, but within eight years replanting had been completed. In the recent war large quantities of Woburn timber went into the Midland collieries.

The country-houses reached their apogee perhaps in the middle decades of the nineteenth century. The greater of them, such as Burghley and Apethorpe, were politically powerful on the Tory side for several generations, so much so that it is hardly an exaggeration to say that they were a part, and an important part, of the government of the country in their heyday. But for all their tenants' dinners and other occasions when upstairs and downstairs mixed (as is related in the pages of Greville's Diary, for example), their owners lived a life apart from the generality of mankind, cut off in their great houses that were surrounded by thousands of acres of private parks, living the life of minor royalty on their princely incomes of twenty to a hundred thousand a year; and the countryside lost much of its savour by reason of this separation. Though they replanned so much of the Midland countryside, making it to their own liking, the country-houses were never an integral part of it as the old squires had been, and still were where they survived in the backwoods. Indeed, the squires were dying out in the Midlands in the face of this territorial aggrandisement of the nobility. When we look through the pages of the *Domesday of Landowners*, compiled in 1873, we see comparatively few ancient names left in the Midland shires. Not many of the original squirearchy of even Stuart times were left, unlike, say, Devon, which still had many obstinate families whose name came from their dwelling-places, or whose manorial village was called after them. Devon was far enough away from London even seventy years ago not to be much invaded by City men, officials, and the new rich generally as the Midlands had been since the sixteenth century. Nor were there many vast estates in Devon to swallow up all around them, as in Northamptonshire.

So it is that in the Midlands the squires' houses—the lesser country-houses—have tended to disappear or at best to fall to the level of farmhouses, occupied by yeomen. Ragdale (Leicestershire) is a case in point: the home of the Shirleys from the fourteenth century to the nineteenth, and then a farmhouse: then partitioned between two farms: and now empty and dropping apart. It is, in the main, the large country-house which is characteristic of the Midland shires, just as in the south-west of England it is the small squire's house that is most often seen, in a small park of a hundred acres rather than a thousand.

The running of the great Midland palaces was an art requiring the most elaborate rules and organisation. Miss Scott-Thomson has well described the household of the earls of Bedford at Woburn in the seventeenth century, that great park and house that was only a portion of the Russells' vast monastic spoils of a hundred years earlier. At the other end of the Midlands there was the princely splendour of the earls of Rutland at Belvoir Castle, and the hardly less magnificent household of the earls of Huntingdon at Ashby-de-la-Zouch, about whose organisation we know a great deal from the surviving records.

Thomas Manners, first earl of Rutland, a title never previously held outside the royal family, inherited Belvoir in 1525. He was the real founder of the vast fortunes of his family in that period of unexampled opportunity for the acquisitive and the energetic, for in less than twenty years before his death in 1543 he had acquired, as a personal friend of the king, monastic properties on a grand scale in many counties, but principally in Leicestershire where his castle lay. Here he obtained the site and all the lands of the abbeys of Croxton, Owston, and Garendon, and of the neighbouring priory of Belvoir, so accumulating the greater part of the thirty thousand acres which the family owned in the county up to recent years. At his death, though he left great debts (probably money borrowed to finance his large purchases), his lands were valued at over £1,800 a year, or some £55,000 in modern (1939) money, so far as we can make such a comparison.

Belvoir was largely rebuilt by him and his son, the second earl, and became one of the most splendid houses even in Elizabethan England. We are told by Gervase Holles, in his *Memorials of the Holles Family*, that his grandfather "became a follower of Edward, earl of Rutland (that magnificent Earle who kept an house like a Prince's Court) to whom he was gentleman of the horse". Most of the officers of the Belvoir household were drawn from gentle families round about, and John Kingston was no exception: he had inherited nearly eighteen hundred acres in Lincolnshire. But he entertained his noble master so liberally that the earl was driven to

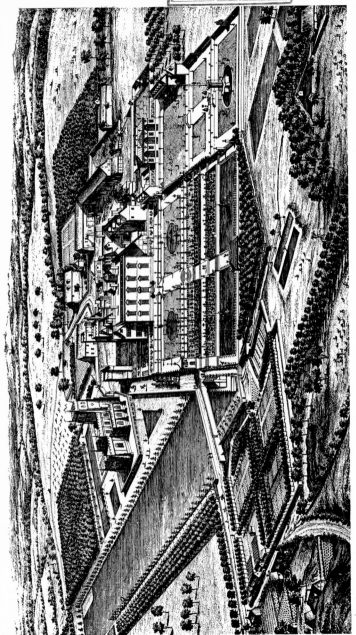

52   Staunton Harold, Leicestershire, showing the Inigo Jones front of the house and the church built in 1653–63
(*From an engraving by J. Kip, c. 1724*)

53 Drayton House, Northamptonshire: the Adam style Dining-Room, *c.* 1760

say one day: "Kingston, thou wilt run out of all thy estate if thou best at such charge to make me welcome!", to which Kingston replied that if this came to pass he could always become a keeper of one of his lordship's many parks. Whereupon his grandson sadly comments: "so little did the gayety of his youth consider what mists would fall in the evening."

The list of officers and servants in the Rutland household, drawn up in 1539, is impressive, from the treasurer and the comptroller— the two most important officers in any great house—down to the scullions. There were chaplains, a physician, a surgeon, an apothecary, a secretary, and a schoolmaster; gentlewomen waiters (Mistress Margaret Paston was one of them), gentleman waiters, gentleman ushers, yeoman waiters and yeoman ushers; a clerk of the kitchen (highly important post), grooms of the chamber, ushers of the hall, keepers of the wardrobe, yeoman cooks, grooms of the kitchen; minstrels, porters, bakers, brewers, stablemen, lardermen, scullions, gardeners, armourers, bargemen, huntsmen, warreners, slaughtermen, smiths, coopers, shepherds, millers, carpenters, joiners, glaziers, carters, tilers, laundry women, dairy women, poultry women; and still that does not exhaust the list. When Roger, the fifth earl, died in the summer of 1612, a check-roll of all the servants "against his Lordship's funerall" ran to more than two hundred names.

Shortly before the fifth earl's death the treasurer of the household had compiled, in 1611, a treatise on the provision of supplies for the running of Belvoir which covers everything from the "beeves" and sheep consumed in the house down to the soap and the wellropes: not even the mustard seed (bought at Stourbridge Fair) escaped the treasurer's careful eye. Belvoir drew upon a great part of the Midlands for its provisioning, and even farther afield—from London, Boston, and Yorkshire. Of oxen, steers, and heifers, seventy were consumed annually. Four hundred sheep were needed yearly, of which "the twoo sheep-walkes" of Hambleton in Yorkshire supplied two hundred, and the rest came from pastures round Belvoir. Forty lambs, thirty pigs, and two thousand four hundred rabbits similarly disappeared into the kitchens.

The mountains of dried fish annually consumed at the castle were bought mostly at Stourbridge Fair, just outside Cambridge, and carried down the rivers and along the fenland dykes to Deeping, on the Welland, "by Deepeing boates". From here the earl's tenants at Deeping brought them by cart to Uffington, five or six miles along the road, where the Uffington tenants took over and brought them up to Belvoir, about twenty-four miles through Stamford and thence along the prehistoric road called Sewstern Lane, the same road followed by the earls when they travelled up to London with their retinue. The dried fish, we are told in the treasurer's treatise, "must be carefully ayred in March and October, and not spent till the third yeare".

Other Lenten provisions came from King's Lynn market and were similarly brought up to Belvoir by tenants, while the fresh fish (carp, bream, and tench) were netted as required in the various ponds near the castle, which were stocked from Crowland and other fenland places and tended by one Robert Bingham at an annual salary of five pounds.

White wine and claret were bought at Boston (five times a year) and, like all provisions bought at Boston, were fetched and brought to the castle by the earl's tenants at Saltby and Croxton, two of his Leicestershire manors. Sack, muscadine, and Rhenish wine all came from London, as did all the fruit and spices.

All the oats and peas needed at the castle, and most of the wheat, came from "rent corn", i.e. rents paid in kind by various tenants, and the rye and barley came from one of his lordship's farms near by. The hops for his beer were grown in two of his many parks (Croxton and Garendon—both formerly the sites of abbeys); twenty-four pounds of good hops were allowed to twenty-one hogsheads of beer, and eight pounds of hops to four hogsheads of "March beere". John Buck, the hopman, got £6 13s. 4d. a year for tending the hops.

And so the list goes on, with detailed arrangements and rules for every conceivable commodity and service that a great house would require, including the rat-catcher, who got forty shillings a year for keeping Belvoir and Annesley (a Nottinghamshire property) free of rats, and was provided with a horse for his journeys between the two places. Slates came from the famous Colly Weston quarries, the other side of Stamford, "unwrought" at eight shillings a thousand, "bored and wrought" at twenty shillings a thousand. The tenants of Uffington brought them to Sewstern moor (again along that old road), where the Saltby tenants met them and took the load on to Belvoir. The treasurer notes that any slates that are needed should be purchased after a frost, "at which time they are cheapest", as they were (and still are) true stone-slates which are left out wet for the frost to split.

On the other side of the county, at Ashby Castle, the fifth earl of Huntingdon was similarly engaged, just about the same time (1609), in laying down rules for the running of his own great household. The results of his labours were set down in a household book which has apparently been lost since it was copied about a hundred and fifty years ago, but the copy gives us a detailed picture of the organisation, administration, and finance of a great nobleman's house in the early seventeenth century.

54 Apethorpe, Northamptonshire: The Long Gallery, *c.* 1623

"Country Life" Photograph

56   Claydon House, Buckinghamshire.
Staircase *c.* 1770

55   Castle Ashby, Northamptonshire:
late seventeenth-century staircase in the East Wing

The form of the book is quite different from that compiled at Belvoir. After a long preamble, which sets out the reasons for making the book, we have the detailed duties of the principal officers and servants of the household at Ashby—the Steward, the Gentleman Usher, the Gentleman of the Horse, the Clerk of the Kitchen, the Cook, the Usher of the Hall, the Almoner, the Yeoman of the Pantry, the Yeoman of the Buttery, the Porter, the Yeoman of the Wardrobe, the Yeoman of the Granary, the Baker and the Brewer. Then follow general instructions to all officers and servants of the household, a statement of the annual budget of the household— "A breefe of all the charges and expences for the provision of my Lord's house"—and, lastly, a list of all the officers and servants of the house by name—"a check-roll of all my officers and servants which are allowed their diet in my house, taken the 20th day of August, 1609".

The preamble runs as follows:

"Certeyne orders and dyrections, to bee observed by the household officers and other persons, servantes to the right honourable Henry earle of Huntingdon, for the better and more exquisite performance of everie man's dutye in his severall place, as well towards his lordship, as also towards the right honourable the ladye Elizabeth countess of Huntingdon his wife, to their most honour and profitt; which orders their Honours pleasure and expresse command(m)ent is to have kept and obeyed from the tyme of the declaration and publishing of them: viz.

"Whereas their Honours, both by the advise of their friends, examples of persons of their owne ranke, and by their owne diligent observations (having some fewe years past ben house-keepers)[1] do finde that nothing is a greater ruine to their estates then disorder, have entred into a dew and mature consideration for the avoyding of the former evill; that thereby their house and family may be well guyded; have determined and hereby sett downe and prescribed to their officers and servants these precepts insuinge, to thend that everie officer maie the more surelie bee established and authorized in the execution of his place, without controlment, for dooeing his dutie, and everie other hould themselves satisfied with their dooeinge according to their orders, and learn thereby to demeane themselves, as well particularly to officers, as also generally one to another. And forasmuche as their Honnours knowe yt to bee vaine, and to no purpose, to prescribe rules and orders, unles care bee therewith had to the obedience and practize of them: therefore their Honnours doe straightelie charge and commande their cheife officers, namely, the stewarde and comptroller of their household, to see the same in all pointes dulie performed: and for the encouragement of those that are tractable to well-dooinge, and the assurance of suche as shalbee otherwise what they are to trust unto,

[1] Henry, the fifth earl, had succeeded his grandfather on 30 December 1604, at the age of eighteen.

their Honnours doe perswade, exhort, and enjoyne all their lovinge
servants, to applie their uttermoste endevoures to the observation
thereof; geeving them heereby to understand, that such as will conform
themselves shall reape the bennifitte of their good favoures; and that
others disobedient (at least wise upon admonition) are to incurr their
Honnours heavy displeasure; and, if they persevere without reformation, to be removed from their service. And for that everie one may
knowe the charge and dutye as well as certayne perticular officers as of
their owne, his Lordship hath first sett down the same. . . ."

Then follow the details of each officer's duties. The management
of the whole household was in the hands of the Steward and Comptroller, who was accountable to the earl himself, and to whom all
the other officers were similarly accountable. He was to keep a
check-roll of all the servants and retainers and their places. The
number of servants-in-ordinary was not to exceed sixty-one, in
addition to four gentlemen. Great care was to be exercised in the
filling of vacancies, especially "that none of the ordinary retinue been
maryed, specially of those that are in any place or office".

The steward should also have a perfect inventory of all "the
ordinarye stuf, furniture, and plate" in the charge of each particular
person, these lists to be checked every half-year, and similarly a
list of all the horses and geldings in the charge of the gentleman of
the horse.

Besides exercising a minute control of every office in the household he also had to keep the household book weekly and check all
receipts and expenses; and if the expenses exceeded the sums laid
down he was to inform the earl and the countess "to the ende order
may be taken to redresse the same". He was to "advise with the
clarke of the kitchin of all manner of provisions to be made for the
house", and to cause all orders and statutes made by his lordship to
be read openly before all the household once a quarter, "that they,
knowing them, may yeelde the more ready obedience".

Every Friday night he called to him the household chaplain,
gentleman usher, gentleman of the horse, and clerk of the kitchen,
or some of them, and consulted with them concerning "all disorders
and misdemeners" of the servants. Offenders were admonished by
him "according to the qualitie of the offences committed", and if
there was still no improvement or reformation his lordship was
informed and the offender was then cast into the outer darkness.

The gentleman usher had to keep a check-roll of all the servants
in ordinary (gentlemen, yeomen, and grooms) and their places of
service, and similarly for all the retainers. He saw to the cleaning
of the dining and "withdrawing" chambers, that the tables, forms,
stools and all other things were set up in good order by seven o'clock
on a summer morning and eight in the winter, that fires had been

lit, and that the chapel was "decently ordered" for their Honours. These duties were all performed by the grooms of the chamber, under his direction. He was also to see that the gentlemen and yeomen waiters attended daily upon their Honours' persons: when his lordship "walketh abrode" there should be at least one gentleman and one yeoman to wait on him.

The gentleman usher must also "be at the chappell in prayer and preaching tyme" and should observe with a vigilant eye who is absent, appointing the usher of the hall to observe also. Absentees with no proper excuse were warned, and a repetition of the offence meant forfeiture of dinner or supper.

If there were guests in the house, he went to the kitchen (a magnificent medieval affair which still stands as a considerable ruin) "to see to the forwardnes of dynner or supper" and thereupon to send warning to the pantry, buttery, and cellar "to make-ready for their Honnors". He also sent word every night to the clerk of the kitchen what bread, wine, and sugar had been used at his lordship's table that day.

The gentleman usher's duties were manifold. After having had his own dinner or supper, he appointed some of the gentlemen and yeoman waiters to give their attendance with him in the great chamber, especially when strangers were there. Among the many miscellaneous rules he was to see that no gentleman or yeoman waiter stood with his hat on his head, or sat or walked about in the great chamber, after the tablecloths had been laid. In other great houses it was forbidden to stand with one's back to the fireplace where the meat was roasting. Once the tablecloths were laid at Ashby the rules became like those ordained for the Sabbath.

There is much more in this fascinating book that one could quote of those leisured, civilised days, but it is time to look at the material side of the picture. The annual budget at Ashby was set down at £2,855 13s. 4d., a tremendous sum, equivalent to thirty or thirty-five thousand a year in our money (1939). It was made up as follows:

Food and Fuel	£1,071	10	0
(including 55 "beeves" and 500 sheep)			
Linen and plate	51	10	0
Rents and annuities	197	13	4
Servants' wages and clothes	210	0	0
Building and repairs	200	0	0
Horses, coaches, etc.	205	0	0
Hawks and hounds	40	0	0
The Earl's apparel	200	0	0
The Countess's allowance	200	0	0
Children's apparel	30	0	0
Attendance on children	30	0	0

Extraordinary expenses . . .	100	0	0
Law suits	120	0	0
Going to London "in the terme" .	200	0	0

Total .	£2,855	13	4

What income sustained this great expenditure we do not know, but certainly the earl's ancestors had been amongst the wealthiest in England in their time. The income of the second earl, for the year ending Michaelmas 1500 had been £1,558 11s. 8d., equivalent to about fifty-five thousand a year in our money; and the earls of Huntingdon had added greatly to their estates during the course of the sixteenth century. Like the Rutlands at Belvoir, and the Bedfords at Woburn, they had to keep a staff of highly paid officials, in addition to the army of household servants, to manage the complicated financial and legal business of the family: in the list of 1500 we find the second earl was buttressed and cushioned by a receiver-general, an auditor-general, an attorney-general, a serjeant-at-law, and stewards for each of the outlying blocks of property, all in receipt of substantial salaries or retaining fees.

The entertainment of royalty shook even a rich peer and some evaded the ordeal if they could. Belvoir, Burghley, Holdenby, Ashby and other Midland houses were frequently the target of royal visits, when the ordinarily large scale of living reached unwonted heights of lavishness and splendour.

On his journey up from Scotland to London in 1603, James the First, proceeding from one great nobleman's house to another, reached Belvoir from Newark "hunting all the way" on 22 April. Here Roger, the fifth earl, entertained him grandly, and among other events Ben Jonson's masque *The Metamorphosed Gypsies* was performed before the king. In the morning, we are told, he approved his contentment by making forty-six knights, then breakfasted, took his leave, and set forward down the old road towards Burghley, where Cecil awaited him in his vast new palace just outside Stamford.

James was at Belvoir again in August 1612. Preparations for his visit began on 26 July—twelve days before the royal arrival—and the household accounts show that forces were mobilised over a great area: even the resources of Belvoir were quite inadequate for the occasion. From London were summoned nine cooks, six "inferior cooks", and a "scallder", at a total cost of £72 for the sixteen days. Another £24 went for "country cooks and laborers from sundry places", waits were engaged from Lincoln, 240 pieces of pewter borrowed from Stamford, and gifts of oxen, venison, fish, fowl, and fruit flowed in from all the peerage and gentry round about "against the King's entertainment".

James frequently visited Ashby also, and the expense of enter-

57   Prestwold Hall, Leicestershire. A late Georgian House in its Park

58   Exton, Rutland.   Victorian "Elizabethan"

59. Claydon House, Buckinghamshire. The Library Ceiling, *c.* 1770

taining him and his court was so great as to impair even the Huntingdon fortunes. It was indeed said that this was James's object in inflicting his expensive company upon the earl, to disable him from making any attempt upon the crown, and the eccentric Lord Stanhope was bold enough to say so to the King's face. It was customary, during these royal pilgrimages round the great houses, for all the neighbouring nobility to call and pay their homage to the King. Lord Stanhope did not appear at Ashby as was expected of him, and his Majesty sent for him and reproved him for his neglect—"but I excuse you," he concluded, "for the people say you are mad!" To which Lord Stanhope replied, "I may be mad, my liege Sovereign, but I am not half so mad as my Lord Huntingdon here, who suffers himself to be worried by such a pack of bloodhounds."

In 1645-6 the Castle held out for the king for fifteen months, a tribute to the strength of the medieval fortress erected by the first Lord Hastings for his own protection, and only on 2 March 1646 did it surrender honourably. The conditions or articles of surrender had previously been debated and agreed by Parliament, so important was this key to the Midlands, and show in themselves the respect felt for a great opponent. Article Six declared "that Colonel General Hastings, with his officers, gentlemen and soldiers, shall have liberty (if they please) to march away to Bridgenorth or Worcester, with their horses, arms and ammunition, bag and baggage, trumpets sounding, drums beating, colours flying, matches lighted on both ends, muskets loaded . . . and have sufficient carriage allowed them, and six days liberty for their passage."

Two years later Ashby was ordered by the Commons to be slighted and made untenable, which was done by mining it with gunpowder. Much of it still stands, however, as a magnificent ruin —perhaps the finest ruin in the Midlands—with its great medieval kitchen, hall, chapel, solar and other buildings (mostly of fourteenth-century date, but some earlier, and a little later); and the great self-contained fortress-house called Lord Hastings' Tower, which has been called "the glory of Ashby de la Zouch".

Belvoir, Burghley, and Woburn still stand intact in the hands of their ancestral owners, though the Tudor palace of Belvoir was rebuilt by Wyatt for the fifth Duke in 1801-16, and after the great fire of 1816 by two amateur architects, the Duchess and the Rev. John Thoroton, the Duke's chaplain. Architecturally, therefore, it is not inspiring, but it looks noble from miles away down in the Vale, crowning its long wooded escarpment, looking northwards over the plain of the Trent. Other great houses remain in their ancient owners' hands but many have changed their life entirely and have become schools, colleges, institutions of one sort and another;

and some have perished. Ashby is a shell, and so, too, is Kirby (51), that beautiful Renaissance house of Sir Christopher Hatton, near Gretton, in the north of Northamptonshire. Practically nothing remains of Hatton's palace at Holdenby, only two gateways and a part of one side of one of its quadrangles. Even those houses that have lived through the vicissitudes of past centuries into the present age of barbarism are hard pressed today, for the enormous estates that built and maintained them century after century have shrunk greatly in the last two generations. In 1883 the Duke of Rutland drew a little less than £100,000 a year from his seventy thousand acres in seven different counties; but when the ninth duke died in 1940 only eighteen thousand acres remained, barely a quarter of what there had been in his grandfather's time.

And even if all the great estates do not shrink so drastically as this, they show their poverty everywhere in gaping thatch, in old slated roofs patched with red corrugated iron, or crumbling stone walls that no one bothers to set up again and skeleton-timbers of barns and cottages. The country-house civilisation, with all its splendour and urbanity, and with all the beauty it created in the Midland landscape, with its houses, parks, lakes, well-kept villages, and fine woods, reached its height in the eighteenth century, and the early nineteenth; and now it is nearly ended. For it was created by one of the most unequal societies the world has ever seen, resting upon the concentration of great wealth in a few hands and on the poverty of the many, and such inequality is no longer seriously defended. It was, nevertheless, a civilisation with great merits while it lasted, and by no means only material merits, and we have not yet found anything as good to put in its place, nor look like doing so for some considerable time to come. But the civilisation of the country-houses itself evolved from a crude, ignorant, and rough society and took centuries to achieve its perfection, and it may be that the civilisation which will replace it, of which there is yet no trace, will similarly take centuries to come to full fruition, if indeed it is allowed to grow at all.

60   Preston, Rutland.   The Manor House, *c.* 1600

61   Toseland Hall, Huntingdonshire.   *c.* 1600

BUILDING IN STONE (ABOVE) AND BRICK (BELOW)

62 Houghton, a characteristic Huntingdonshire village

63 Nassington, Northamptonshire. A typical Limestone village

V

THE OLD MIDLAND VILLAGE

THE great landlord, the country-house, and the spreading timbered park with the subservient village at its gates, are only one side of the Midland scene and one, moreover, of recent growth. Before the sixteenth or the seventeenth century they were not characteristic of the Midlands at all, for more than any other part of England—except, perhaps, East Anglia, that immemorial home of free men and women—the Midlands were mostly a country of "free" villages. Only a minority of villages had a resident lord or squire; most contained a numerous class of peasant proprietors, small owners of the soil whose title went back often into the mists of pre-Conquest days. It is this class of men and women who created the Midland village, whose chose its site, cleared its natural woods and heath, built its farmhouses, cottages, and barns; built its lovely stone church and the mill beside the gentle willow-fringed stream; carved those leaning lichened headstones in the churchyard; gave names to the woods and spinneys, the fields and brooks; trod out the roads and lanes, and built the bridges:

> "Here they went with smock and crook,
> Toiled in the sun, lolled in the shade,
> Here they mudded out the brook
> And here their hatchet cleared the glade.
> Harvest-supper woke their wit,
> Huntsman's moon their wooings lit.
>
> From this church they led their brides,
> From this church themselves were led
> Shoulder-high; on these waysides
> Sat to take their beer and bread.
> Names are gone—what men they were
> These their cottages declare."

It is to these ordinary men and women, and the old villages in which they lived out their sober and quiet lives, that I now turn.

Midland England is more than anything else a country of villages, of compact villages gathered round the church or the green, or strung along a winding street; sometimes perhaps of even more ancient shape—ring-fence villages whose houses, built around the four sides of a hollow square (like the formation of the covered wagons in American frontier days of Indian attacks) reflect the early days of forest and danger on all sides. But whatever the size and shape of the Midland village, we find all the farmhouses and cottages of the parish, the inns and the smithy, are gathered along its streets, and none lie away out in the fields, lonely and remote like those of the wild Devonshire parishes. South-western England is a landscape of isolated farms and hamlets: one may go for miles without seeing a single clustered village: the church stands alone, and the farms and cottages are dotted singly all over the sides and shoulders of the massive hills, and in the deep combes. The parish and not the village is the unit.

But in the Midlands the isolated farm and hamlet can hardly anywhere be found: only in the anciently wooded districts that long remained cut-off, like Charnwood Forest in Leicestershire, and in the old wooded parts of Bedfordshire and Buckinghamshire, do we find farms and hamlets away from the parent village, and the charac-teristic road-pattern of country that has been enclosed direct from the forest. But here, too, the village is still the most prominent type of human grouping.

It is true that even in the counties where the compact nucleated village is most apparent on the Ordnance map, one occasionally comes across red-brick farmhouses in the fields between the villages, but these betray their late appearance by their names—New York Farm, Bunker's Hill Farm, Quebec Farm, Newfoundland Farm. They are the creation of the enclosure awards of George III's day, that revolutionised the old village life all over the Midlands, creating large fields and compact farms, in place of the multitudes of scattered strips in the open fields; but even these isolated farms are few in number, and the enclosure awards, though they transformed the life of the old villages, did not disintegrate them physically. They leeched out all the heart and spirit of the village but left its shell intact.

And so, apart from the industrial districts that mostly lie along a narrow belt of country from the Nene to the Trent where the Victorian prosperity of the hosiery and footwear industries has swamped the old agricultural villages and reduced them to a soggy shapeless mess on the landscape, the Midland village has kept its shape and old likeness. The houses of the village lie all along the streets, mostly facing the street and butting straight on to it without any garden or railings intervening, but sometimes, and usually these are the oldest houses in the place, standing at right angles to it, presenting a blank gable end directly on to the road. The "ancient homesteads", as they are called in the enclosure awards, lay on the village street, or ran back from it; at the back or to one side there was always a small paddock of pasture called "a croft", generally an acre or so in extent (rarely more), and behind the farmhouse was the yard with its buildings (barns, stables, outhouses of all sorts) grouped round it. Somewhere to the side lay the garden and perhaps a small orchard also. All up and down the village streets one finds this constant pattern, with cottages interspersed here and there between the farmhouses, which were well detached from each other; and all over the Midlands, from north to south, this is the familiar pattern—the ancient homesteads clustered within the ring-fence of the village.

In Leicestershire, the farmhouses and cottages will be built mostly of local red brick, especially in the west and south of the county, but here and there in the back lanes the more ancient mud walls can be seen, and less frequently a timbered house of Elizabethan or Stuart times, though these are scarcer in Leicestershire than anywhere else in the Midlands. But the red-brick, which came in generally for village building in the Midlands shortly before 1700 can be, and is, very pleasant in its early styles, with its mellow colouring, slight hand-made irregularities and rough texture, its interesting mouldings and ornament, and the delicate curves of garden walls. There is some excellent building in brick in the Leicestershire villages (e.g. Kibworth, Burbage, Narborough, the older parts of Syston, Packington) and a great deal that is seemly and decent, ranging in date from the 1680's to the 1830's. It is only after 1840 that the real horrors of red-brick as a building material were increasingly explored and, since this coincided with the rapid growth of the two staple Midland industries with their demand for workers, we find in the towns and villages street after street of shiny machine-made brick capped by smooth and shiny Welsh slates, on which no moss or lichen will ever grow: streets and "terraces" proudly dated 1877 or 1884, or some such placid year, rich with lace curtains and large pots of aspidistra blocking the view into the period parlours; streets and roads named after the Jubilee or the Scottish Highlands, or the builder's daughters (Clara Terrace and Laura Villas) or Poplar Avenue which leads briefly to a factory-wall where poplars have long since ceased to blow.

And yet even this kind of building gathers about it at times a nostalgic period charm, with its Gothic Revival doorways and its memories of langorous, unending Sunday afternoons in quiet streets, of parlours that smell of hymn-books and harmoniums and vanished Sunday dinners: and the deep, deep peace of a late Victorian summer evening when the only noises are the distant trotting of a pony and the gritty sound of wheels in the dust. Or is it that one succumbs to this dreadful travesty of architecture, with its somnolent heaviness everywhere, unless one escapes from it at frequent intervals into the loveliness of the stone country, which is mercifully not so far away?

Though the Midlands are mostly overlain with clay, the stone foundations are not far down in most parts. Between the Trent and the upper Welland, covering the south of Nottinghamshire and the south and west of Leicestershire, and again between the Nene and the Ouse, in Huntingdonshire and Bedfordshire, extending into northern Buckinghamshire, the overlying clay is of such thickness as to make the stone inaccessible; and in these districts we find villages built of mud and timber (the so-called "wattle and daub" construction) up to the time of James II, and after that of brick. But in the broad belt of country between these claylands the stone —limestone and ironstone mostly—is near the surface, and here we find some of the most beautiful villages in England. There was a time when every village in Northamptonshire, which is the heart of this stone country, had its own quarry, and probably many more than one, for medieval quarries were generally small; and Rutland is even more beautiful in its stone-built farmhouse and cottage architecture, for it has had no manufacturing industry to ravish its old villages. Hardly a single village in Rutland is not worthy of admiration, in whole or in part, and some are outstandingly good. It is nearly impossible to pick and choose among them, but one might perhaps speak of Clipsham, Empingham, Tinwell, Morcott, the Luffenhams, Ketton (27), and Little Casterton, among the sheep-grey limestone villages (not forgetting little Oakham, the county town), and among the ironstone of the west and south of the county there is the market town of Uppingham, full of good small-town architecture, and the villages of Caldecott (mixed ironstone and limestone), Liddington, Braunston, and Preston (60).

This ironstone belt of Rutland extends back into Leicestershire and produces some good villages in and around the eastern uplands of that county—notably Hallaton, Medbourne, Great Easton, and Bringhurst, and a patch of limestone in the north-east gives us the admirable villages of Waltham-on-the-Wolds and Croxton Kerrial, which are pure Lincolnshire in their style.

The Northamptonshire villages and country towns fall into two groups, according to the stone they stand on: those of the north and east of the county are mostly of the grey limestone, extending into Buckinghamshire at Olney, which is largely built of stone; and those of the west and south are built of the even lovelier ironstone or marlstone, as it is variously called. Where the two stones meet, we get some charming mixed colours as at Gretton (near Corby—far too near) and Moreton Pinkney and at Caldecott in Rutland.

This ironstone belt extends south-west down the long axis of Northamptonshire as far as Banbury and gives some excellent villages in north-east Oxfordshire, of which Adderbury, Deddington and Great Tew are most notable. In Northamptonshire itself it is, as difficult as in Rutland to single out the best, once one leaves behind the boot-and-shoe belt, but Rockingham (69) shows the use of this stone in its perfection.

Wherever you go, however, one thing is inescapable from one end of this Stone Belt to the other, and that is that nearly all the best building in every village and country-town falls into the seventeenth and eighteenth centuries, and that within this period there were two generations in particular in which building was at its height, both in quantity and in quality—the two generations between about 1590 and 1650. Manor-houses, farmhouses, barns and cottages all declare in their various ways this half-century of high rural prosperity for all classes throughout the Midlands: the bay-windows, mullioned and surmounted by that characteristic little gable, appear in village after village and town after town, a style which was most common from the 1620's to the 1650's; and to a lesser extent one finds the mullioned windows, flush with the wall-surface and capped by a Perpendicular Gothic hood-mould, which preceded the bay-window in date, running from the 1580's to the early 1600's.

There is nothing in this farmhouse and cottage architecture which one can confidently date before late Elizabethan days in the Midland stone country, and this, I believe, is true of Cotswold village architecture as well. It seems as though building in stone, so long reserved for the church and the lord's house, came suddenly into use for all classes in the countryside alike shortly before 1600, and flowered almost at once into perfection during the next two generations.[1] The Civil Wars caused a noticeable break in village building and one does not see much that was done in the second half of the century, though towards the end, and running well into the eighteenth century, there was a renewal of great activity, and handsome William and Mary and Queen Anne houses are not uncommon. But these are mostly the houses of squires and, near the towns, of prosperous middle-class tradesmen, who retired into the country with a modest fortune, whereas the earlier outburst of fine building had been largely done by the yeomen, the husbandmen, and the cottagers. These years from the last decade or so of the sixteenth century up to the middle of the seventeenth mark, perhaps, the summit of that true "peasant civilisation" about which George

[1] Leland, in the time of Henry VIII, says, however, that the Northamptonshire towns were even then largely built of stone.

H*

Bourne wrote so well, though he saw, as he said, only the dying remnants of it in his own youth fifty and sixty years ago. For who can doubt, looking at these lovely old houses, whether it is the wealthy yeoman's house or the labourer's cottage, that these old men and women not only knew how to build well, but, seeing how they do it so faultlessly and so effortlessly over and over again, in their barns and outhouses and garden walls as well as in their own homes, that they had an inner confidence, a serenity of mind, a profound assurance of belonging to a great common tradition of life which one can only call a "civilisation", though its arts were humble and some of its customs crude and ignorant. In the words of Ludwig Lewisohn, they were able "to take care of a few fundamental things within the framework of [their] theory and practice —not to take care of them beautifully and nobly, but to take care of them." And so let us turn back to "this elder race", and see what kind of civilisation produced this brief and apparently effortless perfection, however limited its scope; for they achieved results in their building beyond their immediate tasks and aims as though some quality in them was expressing itself unknown to them, as indeed I think it was.

There were two reasons, perhaps largely peculiar to the Midlands, why this peasant civilisation reached its zenith in this part of England, as well as two other reasons that were common to the whole country. First, that the open-field system, which called for continuous co-operative effort on the part of the village as a whole and so gave a peculiar colour to Midland life, was more characteristic of the great middle zone of England than of any other part. And further, that the Midlands, especially north of Watling Street, but to a lesser degree to the south also, were the home of a large class of peasant proprietors, owning from twenty to fifty acres most of them and subservient to no squire or landlord. So we have a social system from early times founded on the whole village as the unit of work and play and government, and on a considerable class of free men and women who owned at least some of the land they tilled.

The cultivation of the open fields was bound to be a communal affair, governed by a multitude of detailed rules passed at the annual meeting of the whole village. There are numerous references in local records to the existence of such an annual general meeting at which resolutions were debated and changes made, if a majority thought it desirable, in the rules. The old system was by no means as inflexible and unchanging as the text-books so often repeat. And any changes were recorded in writing in a book kept by one of the village officials for the time being, and read out in church on the next Sunday or two for the benefit of those who had not attended

64   Milton Keynes, Buckinghamshire

65   Long Crendon, Buckinghamshire. The Court House : fifteenth
century

66 Spaldwick, Huntingdonshire, in the Clay Country

67 Cottesmore, Rutland, in the Stone Country

the meeting, so that no man could thereafter plead ignorance of a new rule. The rules for managing the open fields at Wymeswold, in north Leicestershire, drawn up by a village meeting some time in the early part of the fifteenth century, have been preserved among the manuscripts of Lord Middleton and printed by the Historical Manuscripts Commission, for anyone who cares to read them.

Not only were all the lands of the parish—common pasture, meadows, and leys, as well as the great arable fields—used according to the rules prescribed by a completely democratic assembly, but the village governed itself through its own officials, elected by the same assembly, and every man of any standing and responsibility was expected to take his due turn in the rota of officers—constable (most important of them all, for he was the link between his village and the majesty of the general law of the country), churchwarden, overseer of the poor (from 1601 onwards), field-reeve, pinder (keeper of the village pound), and the lesser offices of village business: every man took an office according to his capacity to serve it well and there are few, very few, references to men who decline to take their share in the government of the local democracy. This combination of a physically unified village, surrounded by open fields that could not be cultivated except by agreed and common action for which all adult persons had some sense of responsibility, was a good foundation for any civilisation.

Not only that, but the open-field system had another important attribute. Besides calling for a truly democratic kind of society, providing opportunities for all men to share in the government and good management of their native villages, it provided opportunities for all, however lowly, to "get on" in a modest way. The man with little or no capital but a pair of strong arms and the will to work was not shut out from economic security and independence as he is today in practically every country in the world (every one, at any rate, that has been infected by Western European ideas); but he had his foot on the bottom rung of a ladder which, with his own energy and skill, would take him, not necessarily to the top (few nourished that restless ambition) but to a level of modest comfort and self-respect, to some sort of standing in his own little society. I have read many hundreds of manuscript inventories of Midland villagers, attached to their old wills from Henry VIII's time onwards, and among these one continually finds men who are described as "cottager", "labourer", or "shepherd" who die leaving a decent competence in worldly goods, to which they had been helped by their own employers more often than not, as the employer's will, when one turns it up, shows. Yeomen and husbandmen, even the more modest among them, not infrequently left to their shepherds or their labourers a few sheep or lambs, or a half-acre or so of crops in the village fields, sometimes apparently not only the crop but the land on which it grew as well.

Out of a mass of such examples I select only two or three: Robert North of Wanlip, near Leicester, described as "cotiar", who died c. 1510 (the record is undated) had "2 kye and 2 heifers" and no fewer than twelve sheep, together with the usual pig, hens and cock which every village family, however poor, possessed.

Richard Straunge of Somerby, a cottager up in the east Leicestershire hills, died about the same time, leaving two kine, a bullock, two weaning calves, three sheep and two lambs, and two acres of barley and wheat, and two of peas. He had, it appears, a cottage and six acres of land (four under crops, and two fallow, according to the three-field system), though his land may only have been rented. The six acres in the open fields, moreover, gave him valuable rights over the common pastures of the village, and on these his cattle and sheep fed without expense to him. He had no farm implements, but doubtless he borrowed these when needed, in return for his labour on someone else's land.

Richard Spencer of Long Clawson, up in north Leicestershire, is called "labourer" at the time of his death in 1561, but his worldly goods were valued at as much as the average farmer's of his time and considerably more than some. He had a cottage, an acre and a half of "weate grounde" and an acre of "pease grounde" (probably an acre or so of fallow, too, which would not be mentioned in the inventory), and rights of grazing over the common pasture for his twenty sheep, four kine, and two yearlings. He kept a couple of pigs as well, and six hens picked around his cottage door.

These are all examples from the sixteenth century, but there are plenty for the seventeenth and early eighteenth centuries, too, and what was true of Leicestershire was equally true of the rest of the Midland counties, as Bedfordshire inventories show in Jacobean days. There is no shadow of doubt that the open field system did afford opportunities to anyone with a good pair of hands, however poor his start, to advance himself a few rungs up the ladder towards security and independence and in this respect alone, even if it had no other attribute, it was a better form of society than that in which most men toil fruitlessly today.

I said a few pages back that besides the two characteristics that were together more strongly developed in the Midlands than in any other part of England, there were two other characteristics of this old peasant civilisation which were more or less common to the whole country in former days, and which were the very essence of the old way of living: I mean its intense "localism", to put it in a word, and (what follows from that) its balanced economy.

As to the first of these, I cannot put it better than George Bourne did in one of his best books, *Change in the Village*. "It was of the essence of the old system", he says, "that those living under it subsisted in the main upon what their own industry could produce out of the soil and materials of their own countryside. A few things, certainly, they might get from other neighbourhoods . . . but as a general thing the parish where the peasant people lived was the source of the materials they used, and their well-being depended on their knowledge of its resources." All over England, country people had this local knowledge of where everything was to be found and how to make the best use of it; and not only did this give them a minute understanding of the soil and of the whole of their immediate surroundings, and a pride for the skill required in using difficult materials where none others were to be had; but because everything that went into them came out of their native soil, their buildings, which are the only remaining sign of that "home-made civilisation of the rural English", look as though they had grown out of the very earth they stand in, so well matched they are and resting so comfortably on it. They belong to it, just as their builders belonged to it and would in due course mingle their bones with it.

To take a homely illustration of what I mean, all the more effective perhaps because it is so small, because it shows that those old men had a use for everything that grew or lay or rested in the ground—a mud wall. If one examines such a wall in a stoneless district, one sees that in fact it rests on a footing of rubble masonry, perhaps a foot or two high, then comes the mud wall itself, and finally it is thatched on top to keep the wet out. Everything in this wall came from the parish or at the most within a mile or two of it; the stones for the rubble footing are rough boulders, laboriously picked out of the glacial boulder clay that covers the stoneless parishes. These had to be picked up before ploughing could be done in any case, but they were not wasted: they all went into the footings of mud walls, or into the plinths of the old pre-brick cottages. The mortar that binds them so stoutly even now was made from lime burnt in the parish or very near it; the mud was local clay mixed with chopped straw and road-scrapings to bind it; the thatch came from wheat-straw grown in the village fields, or perhaps from reeds that grew in one chosen patch—like *Thakkerhul* in medieval Wigston—a spot noted for that one useful commodity. Nothing was wasted. Our own civilisation, if one may so describe it, has a multitude of unpleasant aspects, but one of the most conspicuous, if not the most unpleasant, is its colossal waste of every mortal thing that grows.

As with the mud walls, so with everything needed in the village. All the building materials were local, and some had a more than local fame and usage. The split stone slabs that we call Colly Weston slates are to be found on many houses built between the reign of Elizabeth and that of Victoria, for twenty or thirty miles around the quarries. Everyone with an eye for colour and form knows those mellow, lichened roofs of Colly Westons. But in Leicestershire there were the Swithland slates, hardly less famous in their day than the Colly Westons, true slates from the Charnwood district that were quarried from the thirteenth century until late Victorian days, until they were ousted by the abominable Welsh slates. Mostly they were used for roofs, as an alternative to thatch, and in the eighteenth and early nineteenth centuries they were widely used for headstones. The carving and cutting of these headstones was not only a local industry, it was a true art of the countryside: and whole rows of beautiful examples can be seen in Leicestershire churchyards, extending over the border into Northamptonshire, nearly thirty miles from the quarries, and as far north as Chesterfield in Derbyshire.

Thus, under the peasant civilisation, every parish was very largely self-supporting down to its smallest needs, merely because its people knew the resources of their fields, hedges, woods, and ditches, down to the veriest trifle; but many parishes had as well some commodity on which they prided themselves as having a wider fame, of which they produced a surplus, and this they "exported" to other places.[1] It may be thought that this is a fanciful expression but in fact it is how the local historians thought of their parish when they wrote a hundred and fifty years ago. At Claybrook Parva, on the Leicestershire-Warwickshire border, the curate, Mr. Macaulay, sat writing the history of his parish while the French Revolution raged elsewhere in Europe. He tells us that the "chief import" of Claybrook in his time was pit-coal, as Leicestershire was generally almost denuded of woodlands and the poor could not find other fuel; and the chief export was the excellent local cheese, of which fifty or sixty *tons* were sent away annually, some as far away as London and Leicester.

The parish was a thriving place in those days, with its four thousand acres of various soils "generally rich in their respective kinds". The stiff clays produced excellent pastures for fattening cattle and for the dairy; the gravelly and loamy soils yielded good crops of wheat, barley, oats, and turnips. The same soils were excellent for dairying, for raising young stock, and for sheep pastures. Great numbers of sheep were kept all over the parish and as for meat and dairy produce the parish not only fed itself (nearly a thousand people) but, as I said, exported an excellent cheese into Leicestershire and Northamptonshire and as far afield as London and

---

[1] Most famous of these was Stilton cheese, which was really made in a particular Leicestershire village and merely sold at Stilton on the Great North Road, but there is a multitude of less-known examples. Thus the parish of Appleby Magna (Leicestershire) was remarkable "for a most durable species of elm, called the *Nave Elm*, with which most of the wheelwrights in the neighbourhood were supplied".

68   A Stage-wagon entering Towcester, Northamptonshire
(From a drawing by G. S. Shepherd, 1836)

69   Rockingham, Northamptonshire. Beautiful building in ironstone:
seventeenth–eighteenth centuries

70 Colly Weston, Northamptonshire. Characteristic early seventeenth-century building in limestone

71 Duddington, Northamptonshire. Eighteenth-century building in limestone

Hertfordshire. The farms of the parish, Mr. Macaulay tells us, needed a hundred and twenty draught cattle to work them. No wonder the author comments upon "the hospitality and urbanity which prevail among the yeomanry in this neighbourhood", men of good sense and public spirit "with all the substantial comforts of life within themselves" and no reason to envy any man.

If one goes to Claybrook today to see its beautiful church, for there is little else to go for now, one sees, on approaching the village, not herds of sheep or cattle, or hundreds of acres of wheat and barley growing, but a large notice-board which announces that in the extensive grounds, coyly hidden behind the trees and away from vulgar gaze, stands a *Dog Hospital and Beauty Parlour*. The village that built one of the most beautiful churches in the Midlands; that prided itself on its excellent cheese which sold readily even in London (but only, be it noted, when the villagers had had their fill first—no modern nonsense about sending it all away while the villagers ate frozen and preserved stuff from another continent); that was once the home of a hospitable and urbane yeomanry who envied no man; that village now has a *beauty parlour* for dogs.

Having ventured thus inadvertently into the lunacy of the twentieth century, let us return with all haste to the civilised and rational past and examine a little further the kind of society it produced at its best.

Because the old Midland village aimed at being self-supporting so far as was humanly possible, it found employment for a host of skilled craftsmen within its boundaries, men who lived as much by the land as did their fellows who tilled it and fed their animals on it—the smith, the miller, and the wheelwright (the three most important men of all); the carpenter, the mason, the tailor, the shoemaker, the butcher, the baker, and the saddler and harness-maker. This kind of balanced economy in the old village—and it was an *economy* in all senses of the word to have all these things made or done within the village itself—this kind of economy goes back a very long way, for we find it well developed even in the fourteenth century. The poll-tax returns of 1381 for certain Leicestershire villages, for example, show us a remarkable list of craftsmen. At Hallaton we find carpenters, a brewer, tailors, a barker, a baker, butchers, cobblers, weavers, a cook, a wheelwright, an ironmonger, a shearman, fishermen, in addition to the purely farming households; and at Medbourne, three miles away, the list includes a miller, a mason, skinners, a carpenter, a butcher, and a "belman". Not all villages were as self-sufficient and various as this, but most had their smith, wheelwright, miller, mason, and carpenter, and so it was all over the Midlands. If one village had no mason or miller, he could be found in the next surely enough: there was plenty of inter-village traffic, but in general people found all their earthly needs and wants met within a radius of three or four miles at the most, within sight of their own church spire.

Not only was there this balance of activity within the village itself, but the craftsmen themselves kept a similar balance in their own working lives. All, almost without exception so far as I can discover, had a little land near their homes and farmed in their spare time or when, as was inevitable at certain times of the year, trade was slack. There was no enforced idleness for reasons beyond their control: there was always another occupation at hand, always plenty to do, always a pleasant change of occupation and scene there in the background.

In the old Midland village, for example, the smith was not only the most important craftsman of the community, but often farmed a small freehold also. In the Northamptonshire village of Ecton, Benjamin Franklin's forebears had lived on their freehold of thirty acres since the fourteenth century at least, typical yeomen of the Midland sort, and for centuries they bred their eldest sons as smiths in the ancestral village. The very name of Franklin speaks of their origin as free men. At Wigston Magna, in Leicestershire, the smith frequently witnessed local charters involving the transfer of land in the village, together with clerks, chaplains and other peasant free-holders, and there is, indeed, a regular dynasty of smiths like the Franklins at Ecton. "John the Smith" witnesses a charter made between 1260 and 1274, and "Henry, son of John the Smith", called "Henry the Smith" in another record, witnesses many such charters from 1269 to 1309. For forty years he was an important personage in the village, called in repeatedly as a witness to transactions of moment. All through the fourteenth, fifteenth, and sixteenth centuries we find the Smiths here, witnessing deeds or buying and selling land themselves. In a document of 1515 William Smyth appears among "the men of good credence and reputation" in the village, called in to witness a transfer of property on a more than usually big scale. They were freeholders all through these centuries, right on into the time of Charles II when they acquired the title of Mr.—a clearly understood dignity at that time—and a substantial yeoman farmhouse, though they had long since given up their smithy. Clearly, at Wigston, the smith was among the peasant aristocracy for several centuries, and it was so in all the other Midland villages where there was no squire to dominate the place.

The wheelwright was hardly, perhaps, as exalted a personage as the smith, though he was equally necessary to the life of the village, and he, too, like the carpenter, the tailor, shoemaker, baker, free-mason, and weaver had some land and farmed as a side line. All these examples and more can be found in Bedfordshire villages of

James I's time.[1] At Markyate in Studham, John Carte was the wheelwright, and among the inventory of his personal estate made 29 July 1619 we read "In the shopp & in the yard—all the tymber and fyre wood 21li 2s. All his tooles & working blocks 20s, 3 henns & a broode of chickens 3s, and ould gest cow 30s, and acre & a halfe of tylth in the common feild 6s 8d."

The carpenter at Ravensden, in Bedfordshire, died late in February 1620. Well over half of his total estate of £78 10s. 8d. consisted of his farm goods—crops, livestock, farming gear, and "hovels" or outhouses. He had nine beasts, six bullocks, five pigs, two sheep, ten hens and two small capons; in the fields were an acre of wheat, and 3½ acres of peas already sown, and another four acres "of tylth" waiting to be sown—8½ acres in all. With the fallow of the third field, he had about twelve acres of land altogether.

John Hall senior, the baker in the little market-town of Potton, was a substantial farmer. His lengthy inventory ends with nearly £50 worth of crops in the barn (more than a fifth of his whole personal estate) and "tenn acres of rye growing 15li, fyve acres of wheate growing 7li 10s, and tenn acres of tylth 10li"—twenty-five acres in all, thirty-six if we add in the fallow field. He had four horses, three bullocks, sixty sheep, and the usual pigs and poultry that everyone had from gentleman down to cottager.

The village baker appears quite early in medieval records in the Midlands, perhaps because in many parts fuel was becoming exceedingly scarce and it was a necessary economy to get bread baked down the street at the bakehouse rather than at home. Several Leicestershire villages had a baker by the latter part of the fourteenth century, if not earlier. At Market Harborough we hear of a baker as early as 1232, and at Market Bosworth, "Thomas the baker" witnessed a charter in the thirteenth century. Like the smiths of Wigston, the bakers of Bosworth may have formed a dynasty, for we hear of a series of them down to Elizabethan times, when the name had been modified to Baxter.

The bread made by the village baker was as good as any that could be made at home, unlike the machine-made product of today, made from foreign wheat that has had the life ground out of it in the steel rollers of a combine two hundred miles away, then moulded mechanically, and baked by steam. The old bakers frequently, if not invariably, grew their own corn, just as the butchers raised their own cattle, in the village fields; they milled their own corn on their own premises (usually by means of a horse-mill); and they baked the bread in brick or clay ovens, heated by brushwood and furze, after moulding it by hand. They did everything from the growing

[1] Emmison: "Jacobean Household Inventories" (*Bedfordshire Historical Record Society*, vol. XX).

of the corn to the selling of the bread. Such a man was William Astill, who baked bread for the people of Wigston Magna in Henry VIII's time and through Edward VI's reign into the first days of Mary, and he found time as well to be constable of the village and warden of his parish church. Three hundred years later, the village directory of 1846 tells us that at least one of the four bakers at Wigston still ground his own flour, for Alfred Achurch, who lived in Bull's Head Street, is listed as baker, miller, and mill-wright—a man of parts like his predecessor William Astill, who was farmer, miller, and baker.

And that brings me to another of the manifold aspects of the old village at its best. Its great store of local knowledge I have already touched upon, though one could say so much more about it than I have done: and the acquisition of this knowledge, and the constant necessity of solving difficult technical problems without outside help, or of finding substitutes for some necessity not readily available in the parish—all this sharpened men's wits, kept their minds alive and their hands intelligent. They found a use for everything, even if it was not immediately apparent and they had a sixth sense of the value of the materials they were handling, and of the way to handle them, that it was impossible to communicate to others in words. Henry Peach was the last wheelwright Repton ever had, and the last of a family who had been wheelwrights there since the seventeenth century. When he was well over seventy—and he was always a little chap—he could turn over a five-foot wagon-wheel in his yard, weighing two hundredweight, without any apparent effort, though a man half his age and twice his size would have sweated and strained over it; but he could never have told how it was done, and all this knowledge died with him twenty years ago. What a mass of valuable, hard-won knowledge, knowledge related directly to stubborn facts and to the realities of daily living, has vanished completely from the world with the passing of these old craftsmen; knowledge acquired by laborious experience over many generations of how to use things, how to use one's intelligence on intractable materials; and what mountains of pleasure and deep satisfaction have died out of the world because men have forgotten these old jobs and how best to do them. They were justly proud of what they turned out, these old men, and they expected the things they made to last. One of Henry Peach's carts, made over forty years ago, sold the other day for as much as it originally cost when it was new: but making things to last is another of these ideas that is rapidly dying out of our accountant-driven world. The houses of this "elder race", as E. M. Forster calls them, still stand as memorials of their strength and satisfaction in doing good work, and it is no wonder that so often the owner and his wife had their initials carved over the lintel of the door, and the year which saw the house finished. It was pride in a good job well done.

Every village was a little organism, with a life of its own and a flavour peculiar to it alone, very nearly self-sufficient and always aiming at being so. Around the village stretched the two or three thousand acres which were the basis of its life, the open fields which were more characteristic of Midland England than of any other part. This was the peasant's world outside the few streets and lanes that constituted his village, and he knew every inch of it *by heart*. Outside these fields he rarely ventured far nor, for the most part, ever wanted to. "From long experience—experience older than his own, and traditional among his people—he knew the soil of the fields and its variations almost foot by foot; he understood the springs and streams; hedgerow and ditch explained themselves to him; the coppices and woods, the water-meadows and the windy heaths, the local chalk and clay and stone, all had a place in his regard—reminded him of the crafts of his people, spoke to him of the economies of his own cottage life; so that the turfs or the faggots or the timber he handled when at home called his fancy, while he was handling them, to the landscape they came from. Of the intimacy of this knowledge, in minute details, it is impossible to give an idea. I am assured of its existence because I have come across surviving examples of it, but I may not begin to describe it. One may, however, imagine dimly what the cumulative effect of it must have been on the peasant's outlook; how attached he must have grown—I mean how closely linked—to his own countryside. He did not merely 'reside' in it; he was part of it, and it was part of him." (George Bourne, *Change in the Village*.)

Every slope of the old fields, every corner, every stream and coppice, even a single tree if it were in some way memorable, had its own name in this vanished world, names given sometimes in pre-Conquest days and still recognisably used. Certainly a great number of them can be traced back to the early years of the thirteenth century, when written records become much more plentiful than ever before. *Mill furlong* in Rockingham was so called as far back as 1203, and was still known in the nineteenth century; *Hassocks* in Dingley, farther up the Welland valley, appears in 1199. *Debdale* in Islip is *Debbedale* in 1223, *Flaxlands* in Grafton Underwood occurs in 1240. All these examples are from Northamptonshire, but this continuity was common to the whole of the Midlands until it was shattered by the parliamentary enclosure of the open fields and the usefulness of most of the old names vanished with a stroke of the commissioner's pen.

But during the many centuries they lasted as living names, how they spoke of the rich variety of that old world, recalling the names of owners long since dead and gone, or the wild life that had once flourished in some remote part of the parish, or some strange incident of the past that had stamped itself on men's minds and created a new name for an old acre.

Just outside the village of Oadby in Leicestershire is a stretch of sloping ground, covered with old gravel diggings and known as Brocks Hill. As far back as the middle of the fourteenth century this was the home of the badger, for two documents of that time speak of land upon *Brockesole hul*—"badger's hole hill"—and only a few years ago a badger was taken in the same place. Over and over again we come upon these evidences in the countryside of the long continuity of English life, as when, for example, we stand and watch the crows flying over the hill behind the little Leicestershire village of Cranoe and recall that this is exactly as the Old English colonists, pausing from their hacking and hauling in the virgin woods, saw it in the seventh or eighth century and called it *crawene hoh*, "the hill of the crows". And I have written elsewhere of the pleasure of rediscovering "the black spring" in an outlying part of the fields of Wigston Magna, called *Blackwellesike* in Edward I's time—"the *sike* by the black spring". Having identified this spring, as I thought, on the modern six-inch map of the parish, from various clues in several village charters, I went out over the slopes away from the village, towards the boundaries of the parish, to find it. And there it was on that sunny April afternoon, welling up into a reedy pool that was black from the colour of the soil just there, and I saw "the black spring" just as the medieval peasant saw it when he named it so in the thirteenth century.

The colonists and settlers who gave the first names to villages and hamlets, hills and streams and fields, were sensitive to the slightest differences of slope, of colour, of soil, of plant and animal life: they had the accurate, precise eye for detail of the real countryman. In the eastern uplands of Leicestershire, the highest hill—Whatborough Hill, 755 feet above the sea—got its old English name *hwaeteborg* ("wheat hill") from the fact that its summit, rising out of a great sea of heavy liassic clays, is formed by a cap of Northampton sandstone which produces a light rubbly soil that was excellent for wheat. Though this cap is only a few hundred yards wide in any direction it was sufficient to produce differences of soil that were apparent to the first settlers in this district. In every parish the varying colour or quality of the soils in different places throughout the open fields gave rise to a great number of the minor names of the landscape, and so likewise did the crops or useful wild plants that grew best on certain little local patches. At Wigston Magna, in the heart of Leicestershire, we find a part of the ancient fields called *Blakemilde* in the thirteenth century ("black earth"), another part is called *Brokenbacks* in the seventeenth century after the back-breaking quality of its heavy clay, and the fourteenth-century name of *le Wattrie* referred to some level, water-logged pastures still called Water Lees today. As for crops and plants, there was *Taselhill*, the hill where teasels grew; *Thakkerhul*, where the thatcher's reeds grew abundantly; *Neprodes*, a clearing for turnips; *Goldehil*, where gorse flourished; *Eyl* or *Heyl*, where barley did well, and many other such names. Many parishes had a *Flaxlands* or a *Ryehill* or *Beanlands*, where these crops did particularly well. As for the village of Barton, out in the west of Leicestershire, its bean-fields were so luxuriant that for centuries now it has been called Barton-in-the-Beans. What a lovely scene it must have been in those days: round the village stretched hundreds of acres of beans, climbing all through the spring and early summer until they quite hid it from its neighbours and then, slowly opening into flower, intoxicating the air for miles around with their mild sweet scent; and in doing so gave rise to an equally lovely English name: Barton-in-the-Beans.

Sometimes the origin of a curious name may be entirely lost: it relates to a long-forgotten incident in the distant past and, further, may have been corrupted from its original form by long usage in homely country speech. At Market Harborough there was in the old open fields a bit of ground called *Goodwyns Ox*. We should never have known how this name arose were it not for a record dated some time in the year 1343 which refers to one and a half roods in the east field *ubi Godwynesoxe morieabatur*—"where Good-wyn's ox died"—some memorable local event, perhaps, when Godwin's ox, beaten at last by the heavy Leicestershire clays, just lay down on his side and died at the plough before his owner's astonished eyes.

Other place-names take us back into a world that is now lost. The village of Belgrave, now swallowed up in the northern sprawl of Leicester, was called *Merdegrave* in the Domesday Book, but had got its present name not much later for a reference dated about 1135 speaks of *Merthegrave nunc Belegrava*. The older name tells us that pine-martens (for which the Old English word was *mearth*) frequented the dense woods that stretched even in the twelfth century to the very walls of Leicester. The name of Marefield, a dozen or so miles due east of Belgrave, on the edge of the upland country of east Leicestershire, commemorates the same beautiful little animal which has now almost disappeared from Great Britain.

Wolves went quite early. Although it is said that the last wolves survived in England until the early sixteenth century, I feel sure they had disappeared from the Midlands long before that or the minor names of the landscape would surely tell of their presence.

But among many thousands of Leicestershire field-names running from the early thirteenth century onwards I have come across only one solitary reference to wolves—a "wolf hill" in the early fourteenth century. And even that wolf must have been a miserable survivor, a rare visitant, or the hill would not have been called after him. At the time of Domesday most Midland villages had cleared about half their available land of woodland and scrub, sometimes rather more and sometimes less in the more inhospitable clay country, but the work of clearing was going on steadily throughout the twelfth century and the thirteenth, and by about 1300 I should say most Midland villages had opened up and cleared their lands as far as their frontiers with their neighbours. Small, uncleared, stubborn patches doubtless still remained, left on one side for the time being, but in the main the parish had completed the work of clearance, begun so many, many centuries before, by the early 1300's, and with this opening-up of the landscape wolves must have virtually disappeared from the Midland scene, surviving in ones or twos perhaps in the wilder woods of Charnwood and Yardley Chase. Hence, since the majority of recorded field-names are not older than Henry III's reign, references to wolves are almost wholly absent.

Though the vast majority of field-names were wiped out at the enclosure of the open fields, or when the people who lived through this revolution died off one by one in the nineteenth century, many still live on. As I walk round Wigston Magna today, I see *Ross's Lane*, name of a yeoman family who were farming here from Henry VIII's up to George III's time; *Newgate End*, that was the "new way" into the fields back in 1301; *Bushloe End*, "the barrow with the bushes on it" in the fourteenth century; *Horsewell*, the spring where horses could be watered, so called in Edward III's day; *Goldhill Farm*, a name known since the thirteenth century; *Shackerdale Farm*, which commemorates a remote hollow of the parish where fourteenth-century robbers skulked; and so on round all the lanes and round the fields. But these are only the remnants of the once-rich life of the fields, now so empty of people but in those days filled with men, women, and children, old and young, working side by side at their strips.

The twisted grey hawthorns planted nearly two hundred years ago, the hedges of the enclosure map, fade away; the pasture fields, with their succession of ridge and furrow that tell of former centuries of cultivation by the plough, where the only sound today is the wailing cry of peewits and the creaking of their wings as they tumble agitatedly overhead, these too, all fade away; and the mind's eye sees instead fields infested with children and populous with men with scythes and women following after them binding; fields of white barley growing as far as the eye can see, hundreds of acres of it seething in the summer wind; fields of tall beans and peas, their scent everywhere, bean fields that hide the village, all but the church spire bright with newly cut stone and the sails of the windmill creaking and turning high in the blue-and-white sky: and one hears the cheerful shouts of children helping in the fields, the rushing of the mill-water and the thunder of the great stone wheels as they grind the village corn. It was not all poverty and filth, disease and dirt. Materially most of these people were poorly endowed, but they had a life rich in quality.

Truly it was at its best a peasant civilisation, a rich many-sided culture. It had its darker side: one could enumerate its many faults soon enough; it was far from perfect. But it "took care of a few fundamental things". Men lived in a place that had meaning and significance for them; their roots went down deep into the cultural humus formed by centuries of ancestors before them on that spot; they "belonged" to that place. "Men are attached to places", says Lewis Mumford, "as they are attached to families and friends. When these loyalties come together, one has the most tenacious cement possible for human society." Robert Smyth, who left Market Harborough to make his fortune in Elizabethan London, remembered his native countryside as he lay dying in London, and left money in his will to the poor of all those parishes round about his native town in whose fields he had gleaned as a boy.

Not only did men live in a place that had meaning for them but they worked in it also, all their lives: home and work were synonymous. And, further, they saw the beginning of their work and the end of it and could therefore take a deep pride in doing it well. But their experience was even wider than this, for they saw their work long before it reached them and long after it had left them. The wheelwright on his evening walk was already marking down in his mind particular trees still growing and planning their use in years yet to come; and when he had finished his cart or wagon he saw it round about the parish for the rest of his life and could still feel the same pride as on the day he turned it out, the best he was capable of. This old qualitative civilisation, disparaged and derided as it is by those who have never troubled to understand it, limited though it was in scope, aimed, not at power, but at perfection and now and then achieved it.

VI

THE YEOMAN AND HIS HOME

O F all the tangible memorials of this peasant civilisation of which I have been speaking the most numerous are the houses of the old yeomen, which are to be found in practically every village and hamlet in the Midland counties. Poor indeed is the village that cannot show four or five such houses: the Rutland and Northamptonshire villages show whole streets of them at once, most of them two to three hundred years old, for being built of stone they have stood up better to time than the timber and mud-walled houses outside the stone belt. Away from the stone, however, the south and east Midlands can still show many excellent houses of this type, with all manner of local varieties of design and of different local materials. The old yeoman houses of Huntingdonshire, one of the most neglected of all the English counties, are particularly beautiful and distinctive with their russet-tiled, mansard roofs and their colour-washed walls, a style that extends over the border into Bedfordshire; and the Buckinghamshire farmhouses, north of the Chilterns, are equally distinctive in their own way. For the old rural culture produced an infinite variety of building from limited material resources, because it made the most of what there was.

As the Midlands are the heart of England and the village is the essence of Midland landscape and history, so the yeoman was the backbone of the village community in which he lived, the embodiment of what that rural, home-made culture could produce at its best. In this chapter, therefore, I want to say something about this class of men: their origins, their lands and their material fortunes, their houses and household goods, and a little about their daily lives. One could have written the whole of this book about the Midland yeomen alone, the materials are so abundant and lively, and, this being so, what follows can be only the merest sketch of this class of men, the best and most solid that England has ever given birth to. Perhaps I am a little prejudiced about this, being descended from a long line of such men (though not in the Midlands), six centuries

72   Kempston, Bedfordshire.   A late Medieval yeoman's house
(From the drawing by Francis Stevens, 1815)

73   Sutton Bonington, Nottinghamshire.   A typical "cruck" cottage,
demolished in 1935

74 Alconbury Weston, Huntingdonshire. Characteristic
Huntingdonshire tiled roofs

75 Alconbury, Huntingdonshire. The Goose-green

of yeoman farmers, churchwardens, constables, overseers, bailiffs of the manor, rarely anything much above that, just like their Midland prototypes.

A considerable proportion of the Midland yeomen, as we have seen, were the descendants of the *sokemen* of the Domesday Book and ultimately of the members of the disbanded Danish army who settled on the land in the Midlands from the last quarter of the ninth century onwards. Yeomen of this kind were most numerous to the north of Watling Street, which bisects the Midlands from south-east to north-west. But apart from such ancient freeholders as these there was a further large class of yeomen whose ancestors had been of villein origin in earlier centuries. These had been given their freedom subsequently, and by reason of their greater energy and acquisitiveness had gathered to themselves larger and yet larger holdings throughout the fifteenth century, forming a class of well-to-do capitalist peasants. The fifteenth century was until near its end a time of prolonged agricultural depression in which those with the smallest reserves of capital and staying power went to the wall, and those who could weather the storm emerged stronger than ever, having acquired the lands of their less successful fellows as well. It is these economically successful peasants, too, who emerge as "yeomen" in the early sixteenth century, sometimes (like Latimer's father) having no lands of their own but renting a hundred or two hundred acres from the lord of the manor. By the end of the sixteenth century this type of yeoman, too, had usually succeeded in acquiring lands of his own, so that he becomes indistinguishable from his more ancient brother. There was a vast amount of buying and selling of land in the sixteenth century; it was pre-eminently the century of the country gentry and the yeomen, as monastic spoils dribbled down to them from the greater men and the syndicates who had had the first pick, and as the greater men, frequently in need of ready cash for the building of their Elizabethan palaces or impoverished by the necessity of keeping up ostentatious and competitive spending, were forced to sell off outlying portions of their estates.

The yeoman throve because his major expenses were fixed while his income was rising rapidly. The general price-level trebled during the sixteenth century, but the yeoman, getting ever-rising prices for his wool, sheep, cattle, and grain-crops, wasted nothing on ostentatious display. He continued to live well within his ample means, investing his surplus income in the purchase of neighbouring farms or in the rectorial tithes of his own village or of adjacent parishes, steadily thickening his roots and spreading his branches over more fields and farms. Some yeomen shot up through two or three social classes in two or three generations—gentry, esquires, baronets even by James I's time—but most rose more slowly, buying farms rather than whole manors and advancing slowly and solidly in material wealth though they never rose beyond the honest title of "yeoman".

So careful was the yeoman in his expenditure that his house was hardly any different, until Elizabethan times at least, from that of the much humbler husbandman in the same village. It was usually somewhat larger (an extra room or two—perhaps a buttery and a pantry and an additional "parlour"), but it looked the same from the outside, built of the same materials and in the same way. The great majority of the typical yeoman houses in the Midlands will be found to date from no earlier than the 1560's or '70's, when the yeoman's income was rising so comfortably that he could afford to build himself a more substantial house than the majority in the village without interfering seriously with his investments in lands and tithes. One or two such houses are to be found in the majority of villages, sometimes many more, as in the attractive little country town of Godmanchester (84) in Huntingdonshire, with a wealth of timbered yeomen's houses dating from the latter part of the sixteenth century to about the middle of the seventeenth.

Before Elizabeth's reign the yeoman's house was substantially the same as that of lesser farmers. It was built with pairs of "crucks" or "forks", i.e. two great timbers which curved and met at the ridge, placed at the gable ends of the house, with the ridge-pole carried from one pair to the other. The average house probably had three pairs of "crucks", one pair being inserted half-way between the two end-pairs so as to give extra length. The distance between each pair of forks was called a "bay" and contemporary records frequently express the size of a house as so many "bays of building". Often, too, the crops stored in the barns were measured in the same way, and there are many references to "five bayes of barley" and "three bayes of pease" and so on. There is considerable evidence in the Midlands, too, that the bay was approximately sixteen feet in length, as Addy, in his well-known book on *The Evolution of the English House*, expounded at length.

The method of building with crucks or forks is of unknown age in England: certainly it was well established by the latter part of the fourteenth century. In a Leicestershire lease dated 31 December 1405 the lessee was, amongst other things, required "to make or cause to be made a house upon the said tenement of three pairs of 'forkes' within the term of three years" under penalty of twenty shillings.

It is probable that the oldest houses are those built with their gable-ends to the village street, so that the main front is at right angles to the street and the door well away from it. Every "cruck" house that I know in the Midlands, and these are the oldest surviving houses in the countryside, presents its gable to the roadway. There may be exceptions here and there that I have not yet encountered, but this seems to have been the general rule. I believe further that it would generally be found that even in village houses built at right angles to the street, which now present no obvious signs of great antiquity, the house stands on the foundations of an older one or contains within its walls the cruck framework of its predecessor. Such a theory, if it is true, opens up a fascinating field of inquiry into the origin of this alinement of old houses, which would take us back perhaps to the very earliest days of the village as a settlement; but I cannot pursue this theme here. I can only offer the theory for what it is worth to those who find pleasure in exploring the domestic architecture of ordinary villages and small towns, in the hope that it will lead them to find interest and to make discoveries in the less obvious byways. As a rule, too, I would be inclined to say that the alinement of houses parallel with the village street does not become general until the end of the sixteenth century or the beginning of the seventeenth, so that the odds are that a house gable-end on to the street or road is at least sixteenth century in date, however much later reconstruction may have camouflaged its age. These considerations do not apply to town houses, of course, where the pressure on street-frontage led to the construction of tall, narrow houses with gables on the street, and running a long way back, early in medieval times and where no other alinement was possible ever after.

It is probable that in the earliest cruck houses the forks rested directly on and in the earth. The placing of the foot of the timbers on stone slabs or pillars, or on a plinth of rubble masonry a foot or two high which ran all round the building, was a later improvement, giving further protection against damp and decay and also, of course, additional head-room inside the house. When this change was made is impossible to say. It probably occurred at varying dates in different parts of the country, but I would hazard the guess that in the Midlands it had taken place by the latter part of the fifteenth century, so that houses which show crucks without any rubble plinth or pillar must be attributed to that century, if not to the late fourteenth.

Such houses very rarely survive today. There is one at Cheddington (Buckinghamshire), south of Leighton Buzzard, which is probably medieval in date, though much altered; there was a good example also at Sutton Bonington (73), on the Nottinghamshire side of the Soar valley: and yet another at Hoby, in the Wreak valley between Melton Mowbray and Leicester. All these are perhaps fifteenth century in date. Cruck houses of a later date (say 1500–50) may be discovered here and there in the Midlands, but they are still rare. The post-office at Hemington (Leicestershire) and a house at Thame (Oxfordshire) are good examples from the extreme north and south of our area.

The *cruck* method of construction gave way to the "post and truss" method by the middle of the sixteenth century in Leicestershire, where the shortage of timber (especially of oak, which was the only kind suitable for this work) was more acute than anywhere else in the Midlands, but even in the other Midland counties crucks had been superseded long before Elizabeth's reign was over. Walls still continued to be made of "wattle and daub" as before, called "mud walls" locally, and were not superseded by brick until the time of Charles II and James II. The "post and truss" houses of the Midlands were built between 1570 and 1670, the majority perhaps between 1600 and 1640 if one may judge by the stone-built houses of Northamptonshire, Rutland, and Oxfordshire where dating is easier. A late example of the style (dated 1669) on the eve of brick-building for village houses, survives in a decaying state at Shearsby, just south of Leicester, a fine old yeoman's house now ending its days under a red corrugated iron roof.

North of the Welland, however, few good timbered houses have survived, though one occasionally comes across an isolated example in a back lane or a cul-de-sac which probably owes its survival to its obscure position; but the South Midlands and Huntingdonshire are comparatively rich in such houses and barns. Both Bedfordshire and North Buckinghamshire have many fine timber-framed buildings as they have remained purely agricultural districts, like Huntingdonshire.

Something has already been said of the stone-built farmhouses and cottages which are so numerous in the central Midlands, above all in Northamptonshire and Rutland. These date almost entirely from 1600 to 1800 but are most numerous from 1600 to 1650, the high-water mark of rural prosperity for all classes in the Midlands; and there is a great deal more one could say about them. But it is high time, in our limited space, that something was said of the interiors of these houses and their furnishings.

For many generations the yeoman and husbandman alike had occupied a two-roomed dwelling (hence the three pairs of "forks" that were needed), consisting of a "hall" (or "house", as it is called in the earliest inventories) and a "parlour". The "house" was the living-room, the parlour (so called as far back as 1500) was invariably a bedroom.[1] By Henry VIII's time some yeomen had added a third

---

[1] One wonders whether the older term of "house" for the hall or living-room arose in the first place as a distinction from the other half of the building which sheltered the animals under the same roof. In Leicestershire it certainly seems to be an older word than "hall" as applied to ordinary houses.

77   Tansor, Northamptonshire:
early eighteenth-century building in limestone

76   Duddington, Northamptonshire.
The old Water-mill

79 Kingscliffe, Northamptonshire
Early seventeenth-century limestone building with Colly
Weston slated roof

78 Mount Sorrel, Leicestershire
A remarkable granite-rubble building, dated 1705

room to this simple plan, a kitchen, which represented a landmark in domestic history, and some had a buttery or "spence" in addition.

Thomas Bradgate, the richest yeoman in Leicestershire in Henry VIII's time, had a house at Peatling Parva containing the usual hall and parlour common to all village houses, an inner parlour and a chamber, a kitchen, a buttery, and a bakehouse. He had cushions, feather-beds, hangings on the walls (called "painted clothes" in the inventory of 1539), a fine array of brass pots and pans, "a holle garynysse [garnish] of pewter", and silver spoons and salt-cellars. All these things marked him out from the average village farmer.

His house, however, was only a single-floored dwelling, probably open to the rafters of the roof as there is no reference to lofts in the inventory. By the middle of the sixteenth century it was fairly common to have the ground-floor rooms boarded over so as to form lofts or storage-space above. The records show that at first only the parlour was so boarded over. Later both hall and parlour were covered in, the upper floor so formed being used both for sleeping and for storage, and one went to bed by climbing a ladder which was placed through an opening or trap-door in the boards.[1]

About the middle of the sixteenth century, too, when kitchens were being built on to the old structure and lofts made in the roof-space, the *cruck* style of building gave way to the "post and truss", so allowing much more head-room in the upper floor and making it possible to have a regular series of bedrooms there in place of the primitive lofts. Later still, the structural problem of the fixed stair-case was solved, probably early in the next century. The larger yeomen probably had houses with such staircases by Charles I's time, though they were still rare and I believe did not become common until the end of the seventeenth century even among yeomen.

The inventory of William Collyn, yeoman, of Great Easton, near the meeting-place of Leicestershire, Rutland, and Northamptonshire, is typical of his class and time, and is all the more interesting because his house may, I think, be identified today. On the gable-end of a stone barn in Great Easton, built of ironstone with the usual lime-stone dressings where the wear is greatest, appears the inscription $\frac{RC}{1614}$. RC stands for Richard Collyn, a yeoman who was living in Easton at that time and who died shortly afterwards; and beside the barn stands his farmhouse, a most attractive L-shaped building put up about 1600 (perhaps the wing at right angles to the street

---

[1] An excellent illustration of this type of sleeping-loft (from Yorkshire) may be found in Jekyll and Jones, *Old English Household Life*, p. 61. I know of no survivals of this arrangement in the Midlands, though there is still one in Nidderdale, not a great way from Harrogate.

is slightly earlier) built of ironstone with limestone dressings and roofed with Colly Weston slates.

Richard Collyn's house perhaps consisted of only the one wing, as his inventory, made in 1621, speaks only of a hall, parlour, and chamber. William Collyn's inventory, made five years later, refers to the hall, parlour, "Chamber over the hall", middle chamber, "neather parlor", kitchen and buttery, and I give it here both for its picture of a yeoman's house and its furnishings at that time, and for its dialect words for old country things.

An Inventory of all the goods and Chattells of Willyam Collyn late of Easton in the Countye of Leicester yeoman deceased made and thereof taken the ffowereteenth day of November Anno dni 1626 and the same dulye praysed by John kirke the elder Andrewe Collyn, Willm Collyn ffraunces Dickman yeoman and others as followeth.

Imprimis in the hall of the then dwellinge house of the sayd Willm Collyn One Table half a dozen of ioynte stooles twoe cheares and the ffurniture belongeinge to the Chimney . .	x^s
Item in the parlor of the same house twoe tables one Cubbard and one Bedstead . . .	xxx^s
Item his Apparrell	xl^s
Item in the Chamber over the hall one Bedstead wth the ffurniture three ffeatherbedds one Rugge ffyve Chestes and three hillings . .	v^{ll} xiij^s iiij^d
Item tenne paire of fflaxen sheets ffowre paire of hempen sheetes	vj^{ll} vj^s viij^d
Item eighte pillowebears . . .	viij^s
Item twoe Table Clothes . . .	vij^s
Item twentye Napkyns and three towells .	xv^s
Item in the midle Chamber one bedstead with the ffurniture	xiij^s iiij^d
Item in the kitchin Seaventeene pewter dishes twoe Candlesticks tenne porrenoors one Bacon salte and twoe Chamberpotts . .	xxxvj^s
Item sixe brasse potts	xl^s
Item ffyve pannes and a morter . .	xl^s
Item one ffurnace	xlvj^s viij^d
Item ffoure Tubbes twoe payles twoe kymbdells and aneltinge Troughe . .	xiij^s iiij^d
Item one loade of Coles . . .	xij^s
Item all thinges in the neather parlor .	x^s
Item in the Buttrye one ffatt and ffyve Barrells .	x^s
Item sixe horses one Mare and a ffoale .	xxxiij^{ll}
Item Eighteene ewes and Nyneteene lambes .	xj^{ll} iiij^s vj^d
Item tenne kyne three bullockes & two Calves	xxviij^{ll} vj^s viij^d
Item all the Swine	v^{ll} x^s
Item the Carte geares and plowe geares .	xx^s

Item three Theales . . . . v^s
Item twoe hay Ricks and one bag of hay . v^{ll}
Item the whyte corne . . . . . $xxij^{ll} x^s$
Item the pease and one hay Ricke in the ffeyld xx^{ll}
Item twoe acres and half of wheate . . $iiij^{ll}$
Item Cartes, harrowes and plowes . . $viij^{ll}$
Item hovell Tymber and other tymber . . iij^{ll}
  The Totall Some is . . . $Clxx^{ll} vij^s vj^d$

The Collyns can be traced back at Easton to the fourteenth century. They seem to have been freeholders there since that time, and are typical of one sort of yeomen that came safely through all the vicissitudes of the centuries by virtue of their ancestral acres, surviving as prosperous yeomen in the seventeenth century.

Few of the houses described in the inventories can, unfortunately, be identified with certainty as surviving today, though in the stone-country where houses have their original owner's initials on them and have survived destruction more often than the timber-framed houses, there is a likelihood of identifying a number of such houses with sufficient patience and a detailed knowledge of the locality and of its records. One can often identify the original owner of a particular farmhouse from his initials (I have done this frequently in Leicestershire and it should be easier in Northamptonshire and Rutland) and from this it is a short step to unearthing his will. And with luck one will get his inventory, too, showing the lay-out of the house as it was when it was first built; its subsequent structural changes can often be traced then from the inventories of the descendants of the first owner. But it is rare to find both the house and the inventories surviving. Either the house still stands and the inventories have perished or been lost; or, more often still, one can trace a particular house through perhaps two centuries of inventories and note its structural growth as well as the changes in its furnishings, but the house itself will have vanished.

By the 1680's brick began to supplant the timber-framed house with its mud walls, and there are hundreds of handsome red-brick yeoman-houses to be found all over the Midlands to the north and south of the stone belt, built between the closing years of the seventeenth century and the early nineteenth. The yeoman's house grew in size and amenities also, and was more comfortably furnished as the eighteenth century went on. Clocks, mirrors, good silver, books, cushions, and carpets make their appearance more frequently in the inventories. But the yeoman did not forget his principal business in life with all this comfort: in a great number of Midland farmhouses his bedroom lay at the back of the house overlooking the yard, and not the village street, and he would appear at the window on dark and cold mornings to give his orders for the day to the men down in the yard and thence return to bed until a more civilised hour.

Not many of the old yeomen in the seventeenth century could read or write, and though they were none the worse for that (even better for it, one might easily argue) it occasionally had its disadvantages. When Thomas Wyatt, a successful yeoman of Arnesby (Leicestershire), who had bought in 1609 the manor on which his forebears had long been tenants, was negotiating a marriage between his eldest son and the younger daughter of a family of local gentry, whose pedigree was long but whose purse was short, he was obliged to employ a scrivener recommended by the girl's mother in order to deal with the marriage settlement, as he could neither read nor write. We know of this because the matter ended in a law-suit when he discovered, after the marriage, that he had signed away more of his property than he had ever bargained for, not knowing but that the scrivener was an honest man.

Most yeomen and husbandmen, probably cottagers too, had had some sort of schooling in their early days, and their education was not the class-ridden business it afterwards became. There were, of course, the excellent little grammar-schools, mostly founded in Edward VI's time out of the endowments of suppressed chantries, and many a yeoman's son rose to eminence on the educational grounding he got at the nearest grammar-school. In addition to these established schools, however, which after all could only serve their immediate neighbourhoods, a great number of villages had schools of their own, run by a schoolmaster in the village church, whose salary was paid by the villagers out of the church rate. Such schools are frequently referred to in parish records, or we should never have known of their existence. If I may cite Wigston Magna again, which I have studied in detail as a typical midland village, there was a school of this kind in one of the two old churches from Elizabethan times at least, up to the year the National School came in 1839. It gave the villagers of Wigston the rudiments of book learning for two hundred and fifty years before it closed its doors, and it was apparently open to all—the children of labourers sat on the benches beside the squire's son in the 1580's. Many years later, when the latter had succeeded to his father's estates in the next parish and had occasion to go to law over some property he had in Wigston against several of his old schoolfellows, who were now yeomen in the village, there was little or no acrimony about the dispute. He had been to the same school with them and had known them all well for forty years or more. Like the village government, the school was democratic, too. The only formal schooling the great Duke of Buckingham (George Villiers) had was at the village school of Billesdon as the son of a Leicestershire squire.

The yeoman's children began work at an early age, both boys and girls: how young we do not know, but certainly by the age of fourteen they were able to hold their own in many jobs on the farm. Then came marriage and the formalities of the marriage settlement. The yeoman families married together for generation after generation, forming almost dynasties in their ancestral villages, and hundreds of pounds changed hands between families over the young couple's heads. Often, too, the prosperous yeoman's son married the daughter of a neighbouring gentleman or esquire; no doubt the bargaining was even harder on those occasions.

But before "the cold brood" of lawyers had been called in, the young couple had already been walking long in the familiar fields round the village and the time would finally arrive when they would enter into a binding contract of marriage with each other. In some parts of the Midlands they were said to be "handfast" to each other. The marriage contract in the sixteenth and seventeenth centuries was as final as marriage itself: thus in 1583 the marriage of Nicholas Rawlinson of Burton-on-Trent and Katherine Parrott of Ashby-de-la-Zouch was dissolved by the commissary after more than three years when it came to light that Katherine had made a prior contract with another man. Such marriage contracts were not formally abolished in England until 1752, and before their abolition gave rise to many an interesting suit in the archdeacon's courts, in which the depositions, giving the actual words spoken, bring the vanished years suddenly to life again in a flash, and reveal these dead old lovers for a moment as young once more.

At Barrowden, in the tranquil valley of the Welland, William Fayreman had long courted Isabel Bateson in the time of Queen Mary, and the day came when William desired to bind Isabel by solemn contract in the presence of witnesses. And so, we are told, in the year 1555, "William Fayreman and Isabell Bateson beyng lovers and drawing together", the said William asked Anthony Harrison and William More "to go a little way with him and to here the communication betwixt him and the said Isabell what she wold say unto him". As soon as they were all assembled together, Isabel and her lover, supported by his two men friends, William said, "Isabell, here are two honest men, I trust thy friends as well as mine, and now, Isabell, how sayest thou before these honest men —canst thou find in thy heart to forsake all other men and to love me above all other?" And Isabel answered and said, "Yes, that I may find in my heart to forsake all other men and to owe you love and favour above all other men, so that you may get my friends' goodwill," a somewhat cautious answer which did not satisfy the ardent William. "Nay, Isabell, I will not once set my foot out of the door without I have some promise of thee to ask any of thy

K

friends their goodwills." Then said Isabel: "William, you shall have my love and my favour, and here is my hand and my faith and troth as freely as ever God gave it me. I say ever the same, and ye are welcome to me, and now I trust to God we be man and wife"; upon which they kissed each other and the two witnesses left them to their solitude in the meadows by the darkening stream.

There are many such charming conversations recorded in these suits and I wish I could quote more of them, such as the words of Richard Cotton and Joan Chapleyn. Richard, we read, took Joan by the right hand, saying, "Joan, are you content to take me to your husband and forsake all other for my sake?" And Joan replied, "Yea, gentle Mr. Cotton, with all my very heart." "For this, Joan, I thank thee, and here I give thee my faith and troth and take thee to my wife," and with hands joined they kissed as a token of their marriage. We gather from other suits that it was the custom "at the handefasting" to have a feast in celebration, and "the same night are the two handfasted personnes brought and layed together" weeks before they go to church to complete the ceremony of marriage.

Then follow the years of hard work; the rearing of many children, the almost annual baptisms, the frequent infant funerals; the yeoman serves his turn as churchwarden, as constable, as overseer of the poor or of the highways. He becomes the repository of local knowledge and of village custom and tradition as he grows older. He is called upon to serve as juror at inquisitions or to depose on one side or the other in disputes about the parson's tithes, or the customs of the manor, or the keeping of the fields. And there comes a time at last when he is known as "Old So-and-so", one of the patriarchs whose memory begins to acquire the sanctity of a legal record. When disputes break out over bits of property, illegal enclosure and so forth, and the Crown appoints a Special Commission of local gentry to hear evidence on the spot, what an astounding array of old men assembles from all the villages for miles around to unload their well-furnished minds! There is a Star Chamber record about an alleged unlawful enclosure by the abbot of Leicester at a lonely spot in the country bordering on North-amptonshire, which tells us that an inquiry was held on the very ground in dispute on a Saturday morning in the month of January 1530. The old men of no fewer than thirteen villages, on both sides of the Leicestershire-Northamptonshire border, assembled to testify before the commissioners. Forty-five of them were there, and some had come many miles to that high, bleak upland waste. The grand old man of them all was Thomas Horton of Cold Ashby, aged 85; and there were Thomas Taillour of Welford (81), John Hall of Thorp Lubenham (80), John Iliff of Walton (78), Richard Simmes of Welford (77), and William Smyth of Marston Trussell (74); nearly

80   The Manor House at Warmington, Warwickshire (built as a yeoman's house, *c.* 1600)

"Country Life" Photograph

81 Deep Leicestershire country: Hungerton

all the others were in their sixties, a considerable age in those times.

The old men of the village were important men to the very end, and the memories they recall, as they think back forty, fifty, sixty years and more are full of the intimate detail of history. I like to think of John Smyth of Stoney Stanton, in Leicestershire, who as an old man was called upon to give evidence in a dispute concerning the unlawful enclosure by the local squire of a hill near by, which the villagers protested had been common pasture for their sheep from time immemorial, where they had always been free to take rabbits and hares if they wished without interference from any man. In the course of his evidence, John Smyth recalls his young days, how as a boy "he kept shepe upon the said wast grounde from the tyme he was 7 yeres olde untyll he was 18 yeres olde without lett or contradiction of any person or persons". In the very year that Columbus's ships were beaching upon the shores of a New World, John Smyth sat as a boy of seven upon a granite boulder among the short turf of Croft Hill, high above the blue plain of Leicestershire, looking around the landscape of his own familiar little world, in which he was never to travel out of sight of that solitary green hill through all his long life.

Then it is time for the yeoman to make his last will and testament. The parson is called in, with paper, pen, and ink, and the writing begins (invariably) "In the name of God Amen . . ." and thence through a pious preamble. Doubtless much of this was common form, but a good deal of it is genuine piety too. The will of Robert Forman of Freeby, made 6 May 1563, is full of such piety—"first I bequeathe and recommende my soule into the handes of the lord my god and my bodye to the earthe from whence it came", and "as touching my wyfe with whom I coupled my selfe in the feare of god" he makes various bequests. "If my wyfe be withe chylde whereof she is uncertayne and yf it happen that she be wth chyld I bequeathe to it v^{li} yf god send it lyfe and christendome, yf god do take it I do geve it [i.e. the five pounds] to my wyfe." Among other bequests he left twenty pence to four poor widows on the day of his burial. Nearly every yeoman and husbandman left something to the "poor man's boxe" in the church, or twopennyworth of bread to every cottage household, or some similar gift to the poor of his own village. One midland parson in 1558 left to every one of his parishioners who farmed land as much timber as would make a plough for each of them, and to every householder in the village without exception three pennyworth of bread, and to everyone present at his burial eightpence each, together with meat and drink.

The funeral feast was not neglected: most men made some provision for it in their wills—in bread, meat, and ale. And yet

K*

the funeral expenses were modest enough for the average villager, yeoman or otherwise, something between six shilings and fifteen shillings, including the feast in which the greater part of the village joined. One commonly reads of 6s. 8d. for the funeral expenses at the bottom of the inventory in Elizabethan times, perhaps as much as 13s. 4d. for a well-to-do yeoman. There was no coffin, nothing but a shroud and the parish bier, wheeled to the church by his fellows. Or perhaps even more simply he was carried shoulder-high by a few friends, to the church where he had been brought as a squalling infant, and had later walked as a bridegroom, and then so many times to the baptisms, weddings, and funerals of his children, until he himself is laid to rest with all his ancestors. As one comes out of the little church door at Covington, for example, in the remote country where Huntingdonshire borders Northamptonshire, the churchyard path is lined with the tombs of the Fairey family, the oldest of one who was alive in the time of the Civil Wars, while the latest saw the dawn of the twentieth century.

The parish register at Appleby Magna (Leicestershire) had a note made as long ago as 1670 recording the burial of John Mould the elder under a stone in a particular part of the churchyard, going on to record the names of six generations of Moulds under that self-same stone "and how many before is not knowne". In Cosby churchyard (Leicestershire) there were headstones to seven genera-tions of the ancient yeoman family of Armston—all John Armstons, back to the John who was alive in Queen Elizabeth's time, and many more John Armstons before that sleep "their morningless and unawakening sleep" unrecorded by any stone. The old yeoman was literally gathered to his fathers when his own day was over. Truly a man felt "at home" in such a stable world, living all his life in the same house, the same village, working at the same trade as his father and grandfather before him, dying, it may be, in the very bed in which he had been born. He was an essential part of an ancient pattern of living. And when he died people were conscious of the gap his passing made: he was missed as a presence in the old village because he had played a good part in it all his life, and because he had been an original, a man with his own flavour and personality.

VII

COUNTRY MATTERS

BEFORE the war the Midland shires were very largely broad pastures, some of them the richest in the world, and the finest hunting country in the world as well: all the great hunts are found here—the Quorn, the Pytchley, Fernie's, the Cottesmore, the Belvoir. These are "the Shires", grazed over for three, four, and even five hundred years, laid down to sheep and cattle pastures for the most part in the fifteenth and sixteenth centuries. Leicestershire is the hunting county and the man who has hunted in this county is spoilt for any other, but the Pytchley country in Northamptonshire is hardly less notable (5, 6).

That practical man, Defoe, however, saw these pastures in Queen Anne's time as "a vast magazine of wool for the rest of the nation", all the way from the banks of the Trent down to the Ouse in Bedfordshire. Not only sheep: these lands fed too the largest horses in England, the great black coach horses and dray horses that went up in multitudes to the streets of eighteenth-century London. Most of the Leicestershire gentlemen were graziers and "the graziers are so rich, that they grow gentlemen: 'tis not an uncommon thing for graziers here to rent farms from 500^l· to two thousand pounds a year rent". The meadows of the Welland, Nene, and Ouse were filled with numberless cattle and sheep, "one of the most agreeable sights of its kind in the world," and so they still are.

Ever since the seventeenth century the local cheeses of the Leicestershire pastures were famous and had a ready sale as far afield as London. Greatest of all was the magnificent Stilton, which was made in Leicestershire and sold at the Bell Inn at Stilton, on the Great North Road. Since the origin of this famous cheese is from time to time a matter of controversy, let us set out the indisputable facts from contemporary accounts in Nichols' *History of Leicestershire* (published in eight folio volumes between 1795 and 1811):

"A housekeeper in the family of the Ashbys, whose name was *Elizabeth Scarbrow*, afterwards *Orton*, who married and settled at Little

Dalby about 1720, was the dispenser of this famous cheese, first known in the neighbourhood by the name of *Quenby* cheese; but now (1800) called Stilton cheese, from an innkeeper of Stilton town, in Huntingdonshire, upon the great North road, buying it in quantities, and retailing it to travellers; and it may not be impertinent to notice, that the publick are indebted for it to lady *Beaumont*, whose name is in the title of the receipt."

Monk, in his report on Leicestershire to the Board of Agriculture (1790) says:

"Stilton Cheese is made in most of the villages round Melton Mowbray; but I found it impossible to get at the *secret* of making it from the dairy people. . . . There is no doubt but these cheeses requires a great deal of care and attention, owing, I should suppose, to their richness and thickness. They run from 8 to 16 or 18 pounds, very seldom larger, and are sold at 1ˢ a pound (most of the inns in the county retail them, the price 13ᵈ and 14ᵈ per pound)— In respect to the *grand secret* of making Stilton cheese, I should have left the county without acquiring the process, if it had not been for the politeness and attention of Major Cheselden, of Somerby, who, upon my acquainting him with my disappointment, kindly undertook to procure it for me from one of his tenants, who was amongst the first for making it. The following is the receipt:

" 'Take the night's cream, and put it to the morning's new milk, with the rennet; when the curd is come, it is not to be broke, as is done with other cheeses; but take it out with a soil-dish altogether, and place it in a sieve to drain gradually; and, as it drains, keep gradually pressing it till it becomes firm and dry; then place it in a wooden hoop; afterwards to be kept dry on boards, turned frequently, with cloth binders round it, which are to be tightened as occasion requires. N.B. The dairy-maid must not be disheartened if she does not succeed perfectly in her first attempt.'

"In the dairies which I visited, the cheeses, after being taken out of the wooden hoop, were bound tight round with a cloth, which cloth was changed every day until the cheese became firm enough to support itself; after the cloth was taken off, they were rubbed every day all over, for two or three months, with a brush; and if the weather is damp or moist, twice a day (and, even before the cloth was taken off, the top and bottom was well rubbed every day)—I was informed by the maker, that they were never better for the table than at a year old, but I believe they are seldom out so soon."

Elsewhere, in writing of Little Dalby in his *History*, Nichols gives further details on the subject:

" 'This lordship', he says, 'is remarkable for having first made the best cheese perhaps in the world, commonly known by the name of Stilton cheese, from its having been originally bought up, and made known, by Cowper Thornhill, the landlord of the Bell-inn at Stilton. It began to be made here by Mrs. Orton about

the year 1730 in small quantities, for at first it was supposed that it
could be made only from the milk of those cows which fed in one close,
now called *Orton's Close*; but this was afterwards found to be an error.
In 1756 it was made only by three persons, and that in small quantities
but it is now made, not only from one, but from almost every close
in this parish, and in many of the neighbouring ones. It is well known
that this sort of cheese is made in the shape, and of the size, of a collar
of brawn. It is extremely rich, because they mix among the new milk
as much cream as it will bear. It requires much care and attendance,
and, being in great request, it fetches 10d a pound on the spot, and
1s in the London markets.' A commentator, in two footnotes, corrects
this account slightly. He points out that Mrs. Orton had been housekeeper to the Ashbys at Quenby, as we have already seen, 'where she
had been accustomed to see this species of cheese made, for family use,
under the name of *Lady Beaumont's cheese*', and that in size and shape it
was much more like 'a child's Bartholomew-fair drum'.''

Stilton cheese can be traced back therefore to the first years of
the eighteenth century, to the dairy of that beautiful Jacobean house
of Quenby in East Leicestershire, and its manufacture spread very
slowly at first. By the end of the century it was being made in most
of the villages on that side of the county, and already the honour of
having first created its perfection was claimed by various old ladies
in different places. Even Elizabeth Scarbrow, later Mrs. Orton,
does not seem to have been the "onlie true begetter"; but who the
Lady Beaumont was whose name was first given to the cheese, I
have not been able to discover with certainty. The Beaumonts were
among the wealthiest of the Leicestershire squires, seated at Cole
Orton and at Stoughton, so that the credit in any event still remains
with the Leicestershire pastures. Sir George Beaumont, the seventh
baronet, was a great patron of the arts, friend of Wordsworth,
Coleridge, Benjamin Haydon, and David Wilkie, and one of the
founders of the National Gallery: but perhaps Lady Beaumont was
a greater benefactor to the human race.

Assuming, as I think is most likely, that the Lady Beaumont in
question had been a guest of the Ashbys at Quenby in Elizabeth
Scarbrow's early days there, or a little before, there are two ladies
who could claim the honour. It could be Mary, the daughter of
Sir Erasmus de la Fontaine of Kirby Bellars (whose handsome
Jacobean manor-house still faces the Leicester–Melton road) who
married Thomas Beaumont of Cole Orton, Viscount Beaumont of
Swords in Ireland; or it could be her contemporary Elizabeth, wife
of Sir Henry Beaumont of Stoughton, just outside Leicester. The
latter came of an ancient Warwickshire family. Both these Lady
Beaumonts were living in the early years of the eighteenth century,
and of the two I plump for Mary, born at Kirby Bellars, only seven

miles from Quenby where she must have been a visitor from her childhood. Kirby Bellars is, and has been since the sixteenth and seventeenth centuries, rich grazing land like Quenby's fields, admirably suited to producing such a cheese. Until better evidence is forthcoming, then, I believe that Stilton cheese was first created in the second half of the seventeenth century at Kirby Bellars, in the house of Sir Erasmus de la Fontaine, for family use, that the recipe was passed on as a great favour to Quenby, and from there Mrs. Orton carried it to the outer world at Little Dalby, whence it spread over many villages in eastern Leicestershire before the end of the eighteenth century. Southern Leicestershire produced excellent red cheeses in the eighteenth and nineteenth centuries and many villages were locally famous for their particular product. Mr. Monk, indeed, preferred some of these less-known cheeses to Stilton, when he made his leisurely rounds of the villages preparing his report for the new Board of Agriculture.

These local products of the old villages gave a highly individual flavour to their regions. One finds them everywhere in the days before the village economy was disintegrated by enclosures, machine industry, and railways, contributing to the needs of their respective localities but generally having no wider sale. The dried-apple trade of Finedon in Northamptonshire was one of the most curious of these; it flourished particularly in the early decades of the last century. At King's Cliffe (79), a straggling stone-village in Rockingham Forest, the old wood-turning industry survived in a feeble way into the twentieth century. When Morton was writing his *Natural History of Northamptonshire*, early in the eighteenth century, more than twenty craftsmen were turning wooden dishes and spoons, which were sold chiefly at the King's Cliffe Fair, one of the hundreds of little local fairs that were of immense importance to their neighbourhoods in their day but are now no more. As late as the 1860's there were forty or fifty wood-turners at work at King's Cliffe; ten only remained in the early years of this century, and now there are none. The trade was killed by cheap German woodware.

Another highly localised industry that has died out well within living memory after a life of over six hundred years is the Swithland slate industry in Leicestershire. Like the Colly Weston stone-slates, Swithland slates were worked by the Romans for a time: they have been found in pavements of the second century round the Forum area of Leicester. They are true slates, harder, coarser, and thicker than the Welsh or Cumberland slates, and range in colour from a rich purple to green. "The most esteemed variety is that which exhibits a cloudy green and grey colouring, on fine rubbing," says Mr. Albert Herbert, who has made a special study of the industry and its products. Most of what follows is drawn from his admirable essay on the subject in the *Transactions of the Leicestershire Archaeological Society* (Vol. XXII). From the records we can deduce without much doubt that the quarries were revived in the thirteenth century, probably about 1260, for in a Leicester tallage roll of 1271 three slaters are listed among those taxed, and an undated record (*c.* 1260) refers to a dispute in the Leicester Portmanmoot between Warin the Slater and Thomas the Slater. Undoubtedly the slates were used largely, if not solely, for roofing the more important public buildings and private houses over a long period, and a great part of the output of the quarries must have come into Leicester, only six or seven miles away. There are also frequent references to the slating of manor-houses throughout the county during medieval times.

By the seventeenth century, the slates were being applied to a great number of specialised uses, according to their nature and size. We find slate troughs for cattle and dogs and for salting bacon and holding milk, slate slabs for dairy pavings, and slate cheese-presses. Their structural uses were manifold—walls, gate-posts, milestones, thresholds, steps, plinths, window-sills, wall-copings, clock-faces, and sundials. One even finds occasionally whole churches and houses built of slate (e.g. St. Mark's, Leicester, and a large eighteenth-century house in Sileby), but it is an unattractive building material on this scale. On the other hand, it is beautiful in fire-place surrounds in a highly polished state, especially when used in conjunction with a graceful Carron grate such as one finds in the older Leicestershire farmhouses; and it often took the place of foreign black marble in local church monuments during the seventeenth century. Even the waste pieces were used as covers for drains and in field-gateways. The old rural economy wasted nothing, as I have said before.

In the last quarter of the seventeenth century a further specialised branch of the trade made its appearance and flourished for some two hundred years—the cutting and ornamentation of slate headstones. The earliest example of this local art, for such it became within the course of the next two generations, is dated 1673 (in Swithland churchyard itself), and it seems that the trade was carried on from father to son and grandson, as for example with the Hinds whose dated headstones cover ninety-four years, and the Hulls who were working from 1761 to 1834. These headstones soon spread over the entire county and far over the borders to the north and the south, and reached a high pitch of excellence in the first half of the eighteenth century. The earliest stones are amateurish in their lettering and plain in design, but they develop within a few decades the most elaborate lettering which is a pleasure to study (above all the initial letters) and an intricate design round the head and sides of the stone. An old Leicestershire churchyard is a more artistically satisfying place than one ever expects a churchyard to be; there are so many pleasing examples of this local art to be found. It was indeed an art and not merely a craft. "Only where the craftsman goes beyond the bare necessity of his job", says Mr. Noel Carrington, "and adds some decorative element, either personal or traditional, do we pass the frontier into the arts" (*Popular English Art*), and by this test, many of the Swithland headstones are unquestionably works of popular art. Later in the eighteenth century, however, the workmanship became over-elaborate, though still praiseworthy, and is less pleasing than that of the earlier periods; and after about 1840 it becomes as tasteless as everything else of the time. Cheap railway rates and mechanical production in North Wales killed the industry in all its branches and the pits closed in 1887, but thousands of headstones and roofs survive to testify to the beauty of their product. Nowadays those who can afford it strip the roofs of old houses of their Swithland slates and put them on their own architect-designed houses in the suburbs of Leicester. The slates that once covered even the humblest cottages are now a luxury beyond the means of the great majority of people.

These local and popular arts survived, says Mr. Carrington, "more easily in trades which were either beneath the notice of the cultured classes of society or were not amenable to precedents drawn from Rome or Greece," but perished, for example, in architecture with its prescribed rules of taste.[1] When we go eastwards out of Leicestershire, towards the stone of Rutland, we find a similar local art in the beautiful series of headstones in Ketton churchyard and to a lesser extent in the table tombs: and all the churchyards round Ketton show these delightful stones, set up during the seventeenth and eighteenth centuries and emanating from the Ketton masons and carvers. I have already spoken of the masterpieces of wood-carving in some of the Midland churches (though they do not reach the perfection of those of Devon and Somerset), which at their best pass beyond the frontiers of craftsmanship; and in many village churches the corbel-heads approach the same quality of art. One feels that the best of them, done in the first half of the fourteenth century by anonymous masons of the locality, are living portraits of contemporary villagers. I recall particularly the corbel-faces in the nave of Barwell or of Hinckley, next door to each other in the western part of Leicestershire, where one feels as if one were in a portrait gallery of jovial country faces, such as one would have seen every day in the medieval lanes and fields. Other examples of popular art may be seen in early examples of inn-signs, like the Fox at Huntingdon or the Three Swans at Market Harborough especially.

[1] Though there are various artistic mouldings and ornamentation to be found in early village brickwork (say 1685-1700) when bricks were a new material for village building and before their use became standardised and reduced to rules. The careful observer will have pleasure in finding these examples for himself.

82　Summer shade in the Welland, near Market Harborough,
Leicestershire

83　Wayside Churns in High Leicestershire

84 Godmanchester, Huntingdonshire

85 High Summer at Silsoe, Bedfordshire

The alabaster tombs of the midland village churches can hardly perhaps be called a popular art, since they were fashioned by schools of craftsmen in Nottingham and Burton at the commission of well-to-do families. But they are a remarkable and characteristic feature of country churches in this part of England and something ought to be said about them beyond the passing reference some chapters back. The finest alabaster, beautifully streaked, came from Chellaston, just north of the Trent, and gave rise to the schools of medieval sculptors who flourished from about 1334 for the next three hundred years before the quarries were exhausted. There are of course numerous fine effigies in other kinds of stone, and even in wood, before the period of alabaster, but it is far too large a subject to enter into here even were I competent to do so. The alabaster tombs are, however, so numerous and striking that one cannot avoid some mention of them, for they are sometimes the best things in the whole church, and some are masterpieces of their kind. As we would expect, they tend to fall into groups in country churches where a long-continuing family at the manor-house established a tradition for such tombs. Most churches have none: some have a superb series, and of these only a random selection can be made. Round Chellaston and Nottingham and Burton, of course, there are fine collections, as at Newton Solney (Derbyshire), and the Sacheverell tombs in Barton-in-Fabis (Nottinghamshire) and Ratcliffe-on-Soar (Nottinghamshire). The Chaworths at Langar, the Stauntons at Staunton, the Willoughbys at Willoughby-on-the-Wolds, the Pierreponts at Holme Pierrepoint, all these are in Nottinghamshire south of the Trent. In Leicestershire the tombs of the earls of Rutland at Bottesford are the finest collection in the county, but the Shirley tombs at Breedon-on-the-Hill and the Woodford tombs at Ashby Folville are worth going to see as well.

The alabaster effigies of Northamptonshire have been particularly studied by Mr. Albert Hartshorne (in *Memorials of Old Northamptonshire*). They number fifty altogether and range in date from 1365 to 1629; and it is known that others have been destroyed, like those of the Greenes at Green's Norton, a fine series wantonly broken up in 1826. The Greenes at Lowick are a notable piece of carving by the Chellaston school in 1419: Ralph Greene clasps the hand of his Katherine eternally in stone. Few of these lifelike effigies, with their faithful details of dress and armour, are in fact portraits, but some undoubtedly are. The Spencer effigies and monuments at Great Brington are outstandingly fine, and those of Sir John Spencer (1522) and Isabel his wife are the earliest portrait-effigies in Northamptonshire. They are carved in clunch, not alabaster, and are still well-preserved. He was the flock-master, John Spencer of Wormleighton in Warwickshire and later of Althorp, who established the family fortunes and laid the foundations of earldoms and dukedoms. And he is also the direct ancestor of Winston Spencer Churchill.

The Knightley effigies at Fawsley and the Parr effigies at Horton are also probably portraits and are particularly good. The Knightleys were at Fawsley from Henry V's time and built the beautiful Tudor Hall on the site of the depopulated village. When Rider Haggard visited Fawsley Hall in 1900 before writing his classic *Rural England* it was still flourishing on its eight thousand acres, though feeling the effects of the great depression in farming like every other big house; but it came to an end abruptly in 1914 and was sold up. During the recent war, the old house was occupied by the military and its destruction still further hastened.

To come back to our tombs, however, other fine portrait effigies may be found at Stamford St. Martin's (the great Lord Burghley, 1599) and at Marholm, Easton Neston, Thornhaugh, and Apethorpe to cite only a selection. And above all there are the masterpieces from Nicholas Stone's hand, the marble effigy of Dame Elizabeth Carey at Stowe Nine Churches (1630) and the marble effigies by the same sculptor at Great Brington of William, Lord Spencer (1636) and Penelope his wife, both in their State robes. But these are by an acknowledged master of the craft, and we have moved a long way from the ordinary village craftsman whose work one meets with so frequently in going round the midland countryside; though it is work done in the past and very little indeed is being done like it today. Here and there, of course, the craftsman survives: there are still wheelwrights, saddlers, blacksmiths, good country carpenters and others who carry on more local crafts like Fleet the basket-maker at Thame, but they are isolated figures among the younger men who do not understand their way of thinking.

It is always a pleasure to read about these old men. Judging by the parish histories compiled in such numbers four or five generations ago, most villages had one or two such natural geniuses who could turn their hand to anything they had a mind to. I do not believe such natural genius has died out today, but it has far less opportunity for expressing itself than it had then, and country life is all the poorer for it. Nichols, for example, tells in his *History* of "a remarkable self-taught artist" who had just then died (1805) at Claybrook in South Leicestershire (the place that now has a beauty parlour for dogs). William Hacket had farmed all his life, but

"on retiring from farming, he commenced what is called a hedge or farmer's carpenter, which business he followed for many years; but this employment not furnishing sufficient scope for his genius, he retired to his shop, and employed himself in making first curious walking-sticks, then in turnery ware, in making edge tools, and cutlery ware, and doing all the jobs of the neighbourhood, of every kind, and

86   Leicestershire Cattle Pastures

87   The Horse-Fair at Belton, Leicestershire

88   Threshing Wheat at Exton, Rutland

89   Millstone and Mill-
wright's tools, Leicestershire

of whatever branch; in short, nothing came amiss to him; jobs which regular mechanics would not undertake he would execute in every branch as neatly as if he had served an apprenticeship to it. He would make knives, sheers, and razors, and work with equal neatness whether in wood or any kind of metal; mend furniture, and make various articles as neatly as any cabinet-maker. He was a very honest, quiet, inoffensive man, of rather eccentric character; and lived alone among his tools, a kind of hermit's life, in his shop, which none frequented but upon business. . . . He worked upon principles and by methods purely his own; and was often obliged to invent tools to work with, having never had an opportunity of seeing the various tools used by mechanics in different branches, as he always lived in the neighbourhood among farmers. He made his own bed, and dressed his victuals himself. He was of a close, reserved temper; and his features seldom relaxed into a smile, or even into an air of complacency, excepting when some flattering compliment was paid him on his ingenuity as a mechanic. He never attended any place of worship for many years; and it was very evident that he had little or no respect for the Clergy. It was generally understood in the parish, that his splenetic disposition to the Church and her ministers had originated in a misunderstanding between him and a vicar of Claybrook respecting the payment of a tithe composition for his farm, which he declared he had been made to pay twice over; and which dwelt upon his mind with a rancorous feeling which never appears to have been effaced. It is hard to say what his religious opinions were; this was a subject on which he never would open his mind, however closely pressed. He was, however, a constant reader of the Scriptures; the Bible generally lay open upon his table, accompanied with a brown loaf and a cheese, which constituted a chief part of his food. He was buried June 15, 1805."

How refreshing it would be to read an obituary notice like this in *The Times* one day instead of some of those notices of "grave men of sour complexion, money-getting men".

When the Rev. John Mastin wrote his *History and Antiquities of Naseby* (1792) he cited two such "very able and ingenious mechanics" in his own parish, "one in wood and the other in iron". Joshua Ringrose, a joiner by trade, was even then "constructing a four-wheeled carriage to move by steam" and was also "a very able architect and a good engineer, possessed of uncommon abilities". In his own occupation of joiner "he as far exceeds most others of the trade as a master of the business does an half-taught apprentice". As for John Tresler, who was a working blacksmith, he performed with great facility every sort of work of the whitesmith, was an expert in casting metals, a good locksmith for guns, and had long been famous for making steel crossbars for shooting rooks— "indeed there is scarcely anything too hard for him".

Just outside Naseby to the north, was fought one of the decisive battles of English history, on the morning of 14 June 1645, the battle that decided the Civil War. The curious thing about the battle of Naseby is that it seems to have made so little impression on the village at the time. The resident parson did not bother to make a single comment on it in the parish register, and when the Rev. John Mastin was writing his history of the place he could find very little tradition of the battle barely five generations later. Such scraps of recollection as lingered on are therefore all the more exasperating and precious and bring history vividly to life like all these trivial anecdotes. The parson found one old man, one Warren, aged seventy-five or so, who remembered very well being told by his grandfather that he was then (in 1645) a strong boy about nine or ten years old "and was keeping cows in the field during the whole time of the battle; that he was present at the burial of the dead, which was done by country people coming in from all quarters; some were stripped, other buried in their cloaths" in shallow graves that were still visible at the end of the eighteenth century: they were then concave and water stood in them every winter. Not a word from the old man, though, about the battle itself: perhaps he was having trouble all the time with his cows, who would be alarmed at the din and uproar.

William Gardiner, whose three volumes of *Music and Friends*, published in 1838–53, is a minor classic of its kind, relates how he had known in his youth in Leicester an old man who "often recounted to me that both his grandfathers were colonels in the civil wars, one in the parliamentary army, and the other, on his mother's side, in that of the King. He well recollected their armour lying about, and that they used to melt the pitch in one of their iron caps to mark the sheep."

And now it is time to put an end to these country matters which have kept us so long, and to turn to the midland towns and industry. For centuries, the Midlands have been a great barley and wheat country, besides providing some of the richest grazing lands in England; now the factories are as busy and prosperous as its farming once was, although its southern and eastern parts are still almost purely agricultural. Bedfordshire and North Buckinghamshire, Rutland and Huntingdonshire, have no other industry than farming, other than the brickworks whose serried chimneys flank the main railway lines near Bedford and Peterborough (100). And at Ketton in Rutland, the beautiful building stone is torn out for making cement, just as Corby tears out the ironstone, that once built the village churches and farmhouses, to make steel. Steel and concrete, the twentieth-century mixture.

90 Kimbolton, Huntingdonshire. A street of late seventeenth and early eighteenth-century building

91 Fine eighteenth-century building at Huntingdon

92   The Market-hall at Brackley, Northamptonshire
(From a drawing of c. 1830)

93   The Market-place, Huntingdon

VIII

TOWN AND COUNTRY TODAY

TODAY the city of Leicester, by far the largest in Midland England, has begun to think of a population of 300,000; Northampton, next in size, has just touched 100,000. Luton, on the southern frontier of the midland plain, grows spectacularly (60,000 in 1921, 100,000 today). Peterborough, a quiet little cathedral city with fewer than 3,500 people in 1800 is now a busy engineering town and railway focus with 50,000 people. Bedford, a country town with fewer than 4,000 people at the same date, now has 45,000; Kettering, with 3,000 people then, now provides a living for nearly 40,000. The midland sky is pierced by factory chimneys from north to south, even in the apparently purely rural parts— hosiery, boots and shoes, engineering, brickworks, cement-works, blast-furnaces, and steel-works. And yet even in the largest towns the old country nucleus has not been lost. Leicester is still the great market-centre for the county as in the past nineteen hundred years, the cattle and sheep markets are held every week, the County Assembly Rooms (opened in 1800) still stand near the great open market that is such a characteristic sight in all the towns of the Midlands. One notices immediately, too, how clean and bright the midland towns are despite their industrial eminence: on a spring morning they sparkle and glow in the sunshine and there is rarely a suggestion of factory smoke in the air except over belching, flaming Corby (107). The midland industries were, generally speaking, not mechanised and power-driven until the gas engine had been invented, and the earlier phase of steam and smoke that blackened the northern towns had no place here. An early and rigorous enforcement of the smoke abatement laws has helped also to keep the air and the buildings clean. The industrial towns of the Midlands look prosperous, clean, and lively, and their appearance does not belie them. This is one of the most prosperous regions of England industrially, which has never known mass unemployment and poverty as other parts to the north and west.

When the nineteenth century opened Midland England was still almost entirely a farming country from one end to the other: not a single factory chimney pierced the skyline anywhere, nor would do so for many years. Such industries as existed were mostly highly localised (like the lace-making of Bedfordshire and the whip-making of Daventry) and important only in their own neighbourhoods, except framework-knitting, which was the forerunner of the hosiery industry—now the third largest of Britain's textile industries—and was already widely scattered among the small towns and villages of Leicestershire and Nottinghamshire. And in Northampton and Kettering the boot industry was flourishing on war contracts.

But in 1801 only one town in this great stretch of country from the Trent down to London had more than ten thousand people; Leicester, with 17,000 people, was growing fast under the stimulus of the new canals that were being constructed all over the Midlands in these years, but was still a country-town in all essentials. Northampton had only seven thousand people, and the depressing little industrial town of Hinckley (Leicestershire) had five thousand. Apart from these, the towns of the Midlands were compact little market-towns, bustling places full of local flavour, lively with trade and social activities, and of remarkably constant size: they seem to have grown to a population of 1,500 to 3,000 and halted at that point, and the great majority of them have remained embalmed in that state ever since. They are still delightful little towns to find oneself in on a sunny morning, and though each retains still something of its own special flavour (but sadly diluted since former times when life was more local and circumscribed) they all have certain features in common. There is the very broad market-place, where the spacious High Street widens still more at one end so as to accommodate comfortably the eighteenth-century market-house in the middle of the roadway and still leave ample room for traffic on either side. The street is flanked by tall dignified inns and hotels on both sides, set well back and interspersed with charming little stucco-fronted houses, and shop-fronts with bow-windows, green-painted and small-paned; and the name of the owner inscribed above in an old-fashioned style of lettering is followed by such words as "Est. in 1803". And farther up the street, where the shops thin out, there are the wrought-iron balconies and verandas and porches of Regency houses, the homes of the professional people of the time —the solicitors, the doctors and the occasional annuitant or old lady of independent means. Occasionally a thatched and timbered house of a still older century stands a little incongruously between the elegance and simplicity of Queen Anne brick and Georgian stucco; but mostly these broad, colourful, cheerful streets are lined continuously with the beautiful building of the years between 1680 and 1830: the high-water mark of native English architecture. Such a town is Kimbolton (90) in Huntingdonshire, an almost unspoiled treasure still, and Winslow in Buckinghamshire, Potton and Woburn in Bedfordshire; Aylesbury (97), Newport Pagnell, Olney and Buckingham in Buckinghamshire; Huntingdon (91, 93), St. Ives, St. Neots and Godmanchester (84) in Huntingdonshire; Market Harborough, Melton Mowbray, and Ashby-de-la-Zouch in Leicestershire; Oundle (94, 95), Daventry, and Brackley (92) in Northamptonshire; Uppingham and Oakham in Rutland; Thame and Bicester in Oxfordshire; all these are, in their different ways, pleasant and typical little English market-towns that have changed little in the last hundred years. Such change as there has been is invariably for the worse: the pulling down of the lovely brick buildings of the later seventeenth century and the eighteenth in favour of some dull (at the best) suet pudding of Victorian make; the tearing out of the graceful bow-windows of the old shop-fronts to make way for a featureless expanse of plate-glass; the substitution (in the larger of these small towns) of the multiple store and its mass-produced gimcrackery for the old-fashioned family business that usually sold some things at least that had been made on the premises, and took a personal interest in the customer. Worst of all is the invisible change: the breaking of the manifold links between the little town and the countryside of which it was once the centre and the focus. Some slender threads may remain here and there, but in the main the coming of railways to these remote little places ruined them in breaking their "isolation", and now too many of them are picturesque but hollow shells.

If this is hard to believe—and some of these little midland towns, like Thame, still have an air of bustle and life about them—one has only to look in an old commercial directory for confirmation (and what good reading these old directories make, too, for anybody with any imagination at all!). In such a directory, like *Pigot & Co.'s National Commercial Directory for 1828-9*, one sees what a rich and varied and intensely local life these compact country towns enjoyed, what a microcosm they were of the world at large, what an elaborate social structure and interlocking of trades and crafts and professions they habitually displayed, how they catered for practically everything that the community of two or three thousand inhabitants could ever want, and for an even larger number of people in the surrounding villages. I suppose one would not be far wrong in saying that each of these little market-towns in the midland counties met the needs of some eight to ten thousand people in all.

Take Market Harborough, for example, still a pleasant old town to walk around, with its fine church, its good inns, market-place, and excellent domestic architecture along its principal streets: the directory begins with the gentry and the clergy, who all lived *in* the town and not in large houses outside it; the academies and schools, the professor of music, the surgeons, the bankers and the lawyers. There were bakers (one also milled his own corn), blacksmiths, booksellers and printers, boot and shoe makers, braziers, builders, butchers; cabinet-makers, carpenters, joiners, and wheelwrights; "chymists", confectioners, coopers, curriers and dyers; grocers and tea dealers, ironmongers, linen and woollen drapers, tailors, milliners and dressmakers, furriers, straw-hat makers, hatters, hosiers, clothiers and lace manufacturers; saddlers, slaters, stonemasons, timber merchant, turner, brush manufacturer, and some excellent clock makers whose grandfather clocks still tick on in houses round about the old town; brewers, maltsters, wine and spirit merchants, inns and taverns; plumbers, glaziers, painters, cutlers, seedsmen, tanners, coal merchant, flax-dresser, hairdressers, and a veterinary surgeon. Coaches called every day to and from London, Derby, Nottingham, Leeds, Leicester, Manchester, and Sheffield. There is a whole list of carriers to London, Birmingham, the east of England, the north of England, and to strings of villages down in Northamptonshire and back in Leicestershire; and as if that were not enough "Pickford & Co.'s and Worster & Stubbs' *Fly Boats* to all parts of England daily" along the canal. There was a weekly market and two great annual fairs and other lesser ones. And all this tremendous array of professions, trades, crafts, and services, and all this daily traffic and commotion, in a town of fewer than 2,000 inhabitants. The economic historian might well consult the old local directories before being carried away by his blue-book statistics of nineteenth-century progress and so gain an inkling of the quality of the old regional and local life that was gradually submerged in the general commercial welter of Victoria's reign. The old market-towns were a long time in dying, even after the railways came; some live on because they are mercifully still "isolated"; but for all that they are only a husk of what they once were. William Gardiner's *Music and Friends*, already referred to, gives the best picture I know of the rich social, intellectual, and cultural life of one of these country-towns. His recollections of Leicester in his time between 1770 and 1850, and of the social life (especially the musical activities) of the villages round about, are full of delightful pictures of the period. It would be fatal to pick up the three volumes and to start quoting now, for they are as quotable and entertaining as those excellent books of Cecil Torr's, *Small Talk at Wreyland*.

The decay of the market-towns reflected to a large degree the decay of the countryside around them. The parliamentary enclosures of George III's reign struck a body-blow at the old peasant civilisation, a blow that ultimately killed. The economic historians who

95   An early nineteenth-century shop-front

GOOD BUILDING AT OUNDLE, NORTHAMPTONSHIRE

94   The White Lion Inn, 1641

96　Bedford Bridge, over the Ouse

97　An eighteenth-century street leading to the Church, Aylesbury,
Buckinghamshire

look for *immediate* effects on the villages of the enclosure of the open fields and the extinction of common rights underestimate the tremendous vitality of the old economy and its powers of resistance. It is not likely that such an ancient and closely integrated pattern as the peasant "thrift economy" was would crumble at one blow: but that enclosure was a body-blow that ultimately killed the local peasant economy in the Midlands I have no doubt, though this is not the place to argue it. The contemporary literary evidence is overwhelming, and the modern statistical evidence to the contrary is not.

All over the Midlands the remaining open fields were enclosed and largely converted from arable to pasture, employing on an average only half as many labouring families as before and producing less food for the nation. It was reckoned that an acre of common field produced 670 lb. of bread and 30 lb. of meat per annum, while the same acre enclosed and turned to pasture produced 148 lb. of meat (either 176 lb. of mutton or 120 lb. of beef) a gain of 118 lb. of meat and a loss of 670 lb. of bread. Doubtless other parts of England benefited by enclosure but the Midlands suffered in all respects.

Small freeholders were ruined and disappeared; small occupiers sank to the labouring class, and the labourers themselves were reduced from a "thrift economy" which met their needs tolerably well to a "cash economy" which soon thrust most of them on to the poor rates or led them to emigrate. There was less leisure in the world, too, when the old peasant civilisation was destroyed: noses were pushed harder into economic grindstones under the new dispensation. One only has to read parish histories to see what a real loss this was to the old village.

As the small owners fell out the ownership of land became increasingly concentrated into fewer hands, largely into the hands of the great territorial aristocracy in the Midlands. By the 1870's and '80's over one-half the county of Rutland was owned by four families: the Earl of Gainsborough at Exton, Lord Aveland at Normanton, the Marquis of Exeter at Burghley, and the Finches at Burley-on-the-Hill. These four country-houses were sustained by nearly 50,000 acres in Rutland alone. A quarter of Huntingdonshire was owned by six families, over a quarter of Bedfordshire by six families; over a quarter of the large county of Northamptonshire (600,000 acres) was owned by fourteen families: and some of these families appear in two or three midland counties on a large scale —the Fitzwilliams, the Cecils (of Burghley), and others.

Fitzwilliam's Milton was supported by forty thousand a year from some 23,000 acres; Althorp (Earl Spencer) by nearly forty-seven thousand a year from over 27,000 acres; Kimbolton (the Duke of

Manchester) by forty thousand a year and 27,312 acres; Burghley (the Marquis of Exeter) by fifty thousand a year and nearly 30,000 acres; Belvoir (the Duke of Rutland) by nearly a hundred thousand a year and 70,000 acres; and, greatest of all, Woburn (the Duke of Bedford) by £142,000 a year drawn from over 86,000 acres in the Midlands.[1]

In some contrast to these princely revenues, the Duke of Buckingham and Chandos struggled along on £18,000 a year at Stowe, and the Earl of Westmorland on hardly more than £11,000 a year at Apethorpe. The magnificent pile of Drayton was supported by less than five thousand acres of land and well under £9,000 a year, and a number of other well-known Northamptonshire country-houses were founded on between five and ten thousand acres. This indeed is the peak-point of the Midland country-house, the height of its affluence and splendour, and of its political and social influence. Thereafter it is a tale (for the last fifty years at least) of accelerating decay; and as death duties fall more and more heavily on these great estates the house must either be abandoned, wholly or in large part, the pictures or the plate sold; or if the house is maintained on the greatly diminished revenues then the estates decay. Too many otherwise attractive villages in the Midlands show tumbling walls, gaping thatch, skeletoned barns, red corrugated iron roofs and barbed-wire fences, signs of poverty not so much in the village itself as at the distant "great house" to which its wealth is drained away.

The coming of canals to the Midlands produced a number of interesting changes in the last years of the eighteenth century and the early part of the nineteenth. Economically, they stimulated the life and trade of the market-towns they tapped, and they gave employment in all the villages round about just when enclosure was driving men off the land. (One of the many reasons, in fact, why the evil effects of enclosure were masked for so long.) But the midland landscape, away from its three or four large rivers—and the Welland hardly counts in this respect—is sadly lacking in water as an element in its scenery, and the long, intricate, snake-like windings of the canals through the midland hill-country added just that missing ingredient to the countryside (99). The walks along the towpaths of the Grand Union Canal, and along its little derelict branches, are amongst the pleasantest one could find anywhere in the way of quiet and profoundly English scenery; and better still it would be to travel along the canal itself in one of those long, narrow boats that one sees chugging along slowly in line under the beautiful brick bridges with their delicate curves and through the

---

[1] These are *gross* rentals: the net rentals would be much less. The figures, however, do not include any other form of income there may have been (e.g. investment income) and in the case of the Duke of Bedford exclude his very valuable London properties.

98   Tileworks at Moira, Leicestershire

99   Foxton Locks on the Grand Union Canal, Leicestershire

100 A Great Midland Brickworks

101 Fletton Brickworks near Peterborough

rich midland meadows. Mr. L. T. C. Rolt has written, in *Narrow Boat*, an excellent book on such a journey which gives one an entirely new view of the Midlands, a sort of back-door view. His view of Leicester, for example, as seen from the canal, as it winds and cuts between the factories, wharves, mills, and works of all kinds, is far removed from the flattering prospect one gets on coming to it by road from the south, to the brow of the hill on the London Road, where the town lies stretched before one in the hollow, with the blue and jagged hills of Charnwood in the background. On the other hand, Mr. Rolt saw views that one can only see from a boat, beautiful stretches of river and canal that would, he says, have delighted Constable or Cotman.

The canals have had other incidental affects. They have introduced into the Midlands some of the characteristic flora of the slow-moving Norfolk rivers, and transported plants by barge from the Thames Valley, and they have brought bird-life that was formerly missing (like the reed-bunting). The reservoirs, too, that were constructed in the nineteenth century to feed the swelling industrial towns with water, both for their industries and their people, have changed the landscape and its flora and fauna very markedly. The Charnwood reservoirs that supply Leicester (Thornton, Cropston, and Swithland) are particularly beautiful sheets of water filling natural hollows and valleys and highly interesting to the bird-watcher and the botanist, while to the south there are the Sulby reservoirs at the source of the Warwickshire Avon. Eastwards the 400-acre reservoir of the Eye valley, where Leicestershire and Rutland meet, was completed and opened in 1940. It, too, has transformed the appearance of the landscape around it and has attracted an entirely new succession of bird-life already.

By the middle of the nineteenth century the industrial towns of the Midlands were on the eve of a great expansion. Northampton was flourishing still, no longer on the army contracts which go back to the time of the Civil War, but on the export trade to the West Indies and to Australia. The emancipation of slaves in 1833 had the curious effect of stimulating the Northampton trade: the freed negroes wished to demonstrate their new equality by dressing like the white people. They would not go to church unless they had boots, and they even stipulated, in ordering from Northampton, that the boots should squeak, so that all should mark their progress up the aisle.[1] When this trade slackened, the Australian gold rush

---

[1] I have been told recently of a Midland clothier who developed a considerable trade in men's ready-made evening dress with the negroes of West Africa. They stipulated that they wanted only *the front* of the suit and no more. Upon inquiry into this curious request, it appeared that the suits were used for dressing up corpses after the American custom, before burial; but the economically minded natives saw no reason for wasting the whole suit in this way.

M

of 1851 produced vast orders for miners' boots; and if supplies of miners' boots ran out at Northampton, carpet-slippers were taken just as readily.

The footwear trade, now Leicester's second staple industry, began in a curious way. A northern man who came south to start a boot factory at Northampton, found a strike in progress there, returned to Leicester where labour was readily available, and began operations there. From that point onwards, helped by local inventions, the trade never looked back, and Leicester is now second only to Northampton as a footwear town. Leicester specialises largely in women's and children's shoes, Northampton in men's.

Almost at the same time the Midland iron industry was revived after a long silence. Iron-working was carried on in the Rockingham Forest area as early as the eleventh century, but it seems to have died out in the early Middle Ages. Most of the ironstone which yielded the ore was in fact used for building purposes (both churches and domestic architecture) from about the early thirteenth century, though by itself ironstone weathers badly and requires limestone dressings at the quoins and other critical places. Then in 1852, the great tracts of ironstone in Northamptonshire were quarried once again for the iron-ore. The earliest quarries almost invariably replaced the top-soil (or "overburden" as it is called in the industry) and levelled the land, so restoring it to agricultural use. Since 1900, however, and particularly in the last twenty-five years, this has been done less and less, and there are now thousands of acres of agricultural land utterly devastated in the Corby district. Great mechanical excavators tear off the cover or overburden down to a depth of 85 feet in places and dump it in "hill-and-dale". These waste lands, which look like No Man's Land in the 1914–18 war, with the high barbed-wire fences shutting them off for miles, are a depressing spectacle indeed, a visual reminder of the "robber economy" of modern industry at its worst. Yet if one can forget all this, the great steel-works and tube-mills of Corby are a fine spectacle on a thunderous afternoon: batteries of gigantic ovens and pipes, all the mysterious writhings and noises of large-scale industry. Seen against piling thunder-clouds, with its flame, smoke, and steam, Corby is pure Hell (107). And to think that little Rockingham lies so near, a couple of miles away, out of sight below the lip of the escarpment, and the Elizabethan loveliness of Kirby hardly any farther away in its own quiet isolation!

One does not easily associate a large part of the English iron and steel industry with the peaceful Midland countryside. Nevertheless, Corby is only one of the centres, though the greatest. In 1937 the Midlands (as I have defined them, but including Lincolnshire this time) produced just over ten million tons of iron-ore, nearly three-

quarters of the whole output by weight of Great Britain. Lincolnshire is one of the greatest producers of steel in the country.

But the Midlands are full of these industrial surprises: who would
guess that Leicestershire, for example, produces more granite than
any other county in England and Wales, from its quarries round
the edge of Charnwood and in isolated outcrops elsewhere in the
west of the county? Most of this granite goes to the south-east of
England for road-metal and kerbstones: the Charnwood quarries
like Mountsorrel and Groby owe their prosperity to the fact that
hard rock is wholly missing from south-eastern England, that road
construction has developed enormously in the past twenty-five
years, and that they are the nearest quarries to this insatiable market.
Bedfordshire, one of the most peaceful and rural counties in England,
has the largest brickworks in the world at Stewartby, though
Fletton (101), just outside Peterborough over the Huntingdonshire
boundary, runs it very close.

Industrially the Midlands are one of the most prosperous regions
in England, and indeed in the world. Back in 1930 Leicester ranked
as the most prosperous town in the British Empire. This is largely
because of the nature of midland industries, the two largest—hosiery
and footwear—turning out essential consumer goods which will
always be in demand. (Hosiery, by the way, covers all textiles which
are knitted and not woven: the term is really quite misleading.)
More than that, there is generally speaking a balanced industrial
structure in these midland towns: the eggs are not all in one basket,
of which the bottom is liable to fall out, as in so many specialised
industrial areas in England. Leicester is a particularly striking
example of this: here are found three major industries (hosiery
30,000 workers, footwear 20,000, general engineering 12,000
workers, before the war) and a number of lesser but still important
industries like printing, for which the city has a high reputation.
The other Leicestershire towns show much the same healthy balance,
though the proportions are different.

More than that, the great bulk of the workers in hosiery are
women and in footwear, men. A great number of households have
therefore at least two incomes coming in. And again, the two
industries were rarely depressed together, so that there was always
somebody at work in the family in the worst of times; and many
workers who were temporarily unemployed in their own trade could
turn their hands to the other with great facility. It is this healthy
balance that, by and large, made the industrial east Midlands a
prosperous area throughout; and the towns show it clearly. Whatever else one can say about them, and architecturally at least they
are all dull and tasteless, on the whole they are clean, bright, lively
places with plenty of shops, entertainment, and social activity. And

M*

the larger towns have, too, a varied intellectual and cultural life. They benefit by being within a hundred miles of London (e.g. in good concerts) while being far enough away not to suffer from the capital's baleful spread; but they have, too, a strong and long-standing tradition of local and indigenous intellectual and social activity. It was Northampton, for example, which returned at one and the same time in the eighties of the last century the radical and agnostic Labouchère and the atheist Charles Bradlaugh, and persisted in returning the latter when the House of Commons did its best to reject him. One can hardly imagine a town of the same size today (Northampton had only 50,000 people then) returning two such outstanding and unusual members to the House.

Architecturally, the Midland towns have grown so fast and in the worst period, that they offer little satisfaction to the eye. Northampton retains some good medieval and later churches, and a certain amount of its older domestic building, but Leicester made almost a clean sweep of the older town and is now very largely Victorian and Edwardian red-brick, with the usual concrete and chromium added in the twentieth century. Nor are Kettering, Wellingborough, and Luton any better: indeed they have even less to show since they were still small towns when the age of good building came to an end in the 1830's. As for the smaller "mush-room" industrial towns, they are generally dreadful little places, architecturally speaking. Some have fine medieval churches; other-wise, they are deplorable examples of Victorian-Edwardian jerry-building, without even any of that grim satanic vitality of the northern textile towns that goes some way towards redeeming their ugliness and dirt. The smaller midland industrial towns are just dreary from one end to the other, and the only centre of light and life (and even of culture in some cases) is the garish Ritzy cinema in the main street.

Of the old country towns that have not been engulfed by modern industry, the greater number dwindle peacefully towards their end. In Northamptonshire the old cross-roads town of Daventry, once a lively centre of coaching England (hence its local industry—whip-making) added more than 50 per cent to its population between 1801 and 1851, but since then has fallen back to where it was in the 1830's. Brackley (92), away in the south-west, has fallen in numbers in the past hundred years; Oundle (94, 95) is back where it was in 1801 and Towcester (68) nearly so: all of them attractive little towns still with their market-halls and many large coaching inns: but the market-halls are locked and opened up only at great intervals for local concerts, and the cobbled inn-yards no longer sound to the clatter of coaches and stamping of horses. The *George* at Huntingdon (102), still a fine place, once had stabling for a hundred and fifty horses; now it has garage room for a hundred cars. The Great North Road is lined with famous old coaching inns which have survived the collapse of the coaching trade. They have lived through the doldrums to recapture the twentieth-century road traffic, and every few miles (before the war) one could be sure of an excellent meal and good accommodation. But away from the modern motor-roads the coaching inns lie silent except for the sociable local drinking in the evenings. They are still warm, friendly places to come to but they have shrunk back into their own little world again after their few generations of contact with the greater world outside.

Wherever one goes, outside the industrial towns, there are the signs of decay, not always perhaps immediately visible but emerging very soon in conversation with an older generation. Although the forces which started their ruin struck the little market-towns eighty to a hundred years ago it is only in the past thirty years or so that they have changed beyond recognition. The old saddler managed to keep on to the end of his days but his son is chiefly a "Cycle Agent"; the old wheelwright kept going till the end, but his shop is now a garage; the mill may still turn (though this is unlikely), but only to grind for pigs and poultry, and not men. The conductor calls out "Blacksmith's Shop" as the local bus pulls up; we look out and see only a cindery patch beside the cross-roads where the blacksmith's shop once stood. The old rich country life has been destroyed during the past four or five generations and very largely since this century began. Over and over again we see the contrast in the Midland villages: the beautiful medieval parish church (as at Stoke Golding, Leicestershire) and the tumble-down village houses. When I revisited Stoke Golding after the war I thought from the gaping holes in the roofs and the fallen walls that it had been hit by a casual bomb intended for a Coventry factory: but it was not an enemy bomb that had done this—it was the impact of modern ways of thinking on an old self-sufficient civilisation. When I hear of the difficulties of getting slate from the North Wales quarries so that the housing of homeless millions is held up yet again, I think of the buried slates of Swithland, still waiting to be quarried on the spot, or the stone-slates of Helmdon in Northamptonshire; and of the wealth of building stone still in the Midland soil (where it is not being ripped out for cement and steel) waiting to be used. And yet they are carrying prefabricated (the word is as ugly as the thing it describes) houses, made in distant factories, to plant on top of some of the most beautiful building stone in Oxfordshire and among decent old houses built of it two and three hundred years ago. One can only stand and marvel that this deliberate waste and neglect of our natural wealth, our great local "resources", should go on unchecked, above all in our present desperate struggle to keep above water.

Here in Midland England are constant reminders of the rich life of the past, based upon the use of all the natural wealth of the local soil and the labour and skill of local men, and their unfailing sense of what was worth taking care of and what was not: look at the multitude of beautiful, or at the very least, seemly churches, full of good English materials and of English craftsmanship; the water-mills and the windmills, some of them miracles of utilitarian beauty; the timber and the stone barns, once filled with barley and wheat, peas and beans, rye and oats, flax and hemp, all grown in the parish, some barns as big as a church; the manor-house, the farmhouses and the cottages disposed in perfect design and harmony (as at Warmington (80), in Warwickshire, under Edge Hill—a masterpiece of Elizabethan and Stuart domestic building in stone, as the other Warmington in Northamptonshire is a masterpiece of medieval church-building); wherever one looks it is all made of the native wealth of the soil, so far as it belongs to the pre-railway age. Hardly anything one can see, that is over a hundred years old, came from outside the immediate locality.

That is how I view Midland England as I go round it, still finding something fresh that is worth looking at, and that is how I have tried to interpret its landscape and its towns and villages in this book. The Midlands are literally fathoms deep in history—for their Roman life is often uncovered at that level—and unless one penetrates beneath the surface, however little, into this past life and civilisation one cannot understand, really *understand*, what one is looking at. Truly, history is a fourth dimension: it gives that depth and meaning to the landscape and to its buildings without which they make no permanent impression on the mind. And what immense depths of history there can be in the most trivial scene in town or country in the unravaged Midlands, and what endless associations of ideas!

I recall a hideous little public-house on the river-side of Leicester, all chromium steel and black glass, owned as usual by a brewery combine somewhere: up the yard beside it runs a narrow cobbled path between unlovely brick walls: as dreary a scene as one could wish to see anywhere in England. But for years I suspected that this narrow way through to a dingy street behind, an ancient right-of-way, was the actual line of the Fosse Way through Roman Leicester—a line completely obliterated a thousand years ago by the medieval street-plan. This alley was the logical last link in a chain of narrow side-streets that seemed to point straight through the centre of the oldest part of the town to the bridge over the Soar by which the Fosse came in, and the fact that it was an old right-of-

102　The courtyard of the George Inn, Huntingdon

103   Eighteenth-century building at Banbury, Oxfordshire

104   Cowper's House at Weston Underwood, Buckinghamshire.
Late seventeenth century

105   The ruined Post Mill at Tillbrook, Bedfordshire

106   A Tower Windmill, Quainton, Buckinghamshire

107   Corby Steelworks, Northamptonshire

108   Quarrying Ironstone at Tilton, Leicestershire

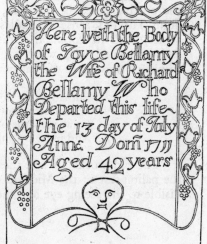

Above) Detail from Headstone at Humberstone, Leicestershire, 1780

Top right) Detail from Headstone at Rothley, Leicestershire, 1732

Bottom right) Headstone at Humberstone, Leicestershire, 1711

From drawings by Albert Herbert, F.S.A., F.R.I.B.A.]

SWITHLAND SLATE HEADSTONES

way, never built over or encroached upon, seemed to add force to what the Ordnance map suggested so clearly. During the recent war, some necessary excavations beside this pathway through the inn yard, exposed the surface of a Roman street, and the chain of argument was complete. The lay-out of the old inn (for it has a long medieval history despite its twentieth-century costume), and of its yard, perpetuated a line laid down just nineteen hundred years ago by the Roman road-builders.

Or if I go a few miles out into the country to the south-west of Leicester, a landscape of clay and frequent little streams, I come to New Hall, a moated site in the fields right away from the village, the home of the Turvills since about 1400 when Richard Turvill built his house here. They lived here for four hundred years, and I have a detailed inventory of the house, with all its rooms and furniture, as it was in 1669, when it was flourishing. Now every trace of it is gone; only two modern farm-cottages stand inside the broad moat. And I think as I look at the site of this vanished house —"the new hall" so long ago—of one of the Turvills who died here in 1506, lord of seven manors, wealthy and deep-rooted in the county of his Norman ancestors. In his will he leaves to William, "my son and heir apparent" a basin and ewer of silver "to go as an heirloom as long as the world endureth".

Now the Turvills and their house, the silver plate and the coaches, the grazing herds in the park, all are clean gone. One contrasts John Turvill's sense of endless security, of his ordered country society with its common traditions and civilisation going on for ever and ever, with what has happened since his time; and one thinks of those lines of Matthew Arnold:

> But slow that tide of common thought
> Which bathed our life, retired;
> Slow, slow the old world wore to nought
> And pulse by pulse expired.

"The old world" is still there, written over again and again in the palimpsest of the Midland countryside and its towns, but still visible to the seeing eye and the sympathetic mind.

INDEX

The numerals in heavy type denote the *figure numbers* of the illustrations.

9 leg

29. May

10¹⁄₂ 6

06/1/50

2¹²⁄₅₀

4¹⁰⁄₅₀

31/10/50

AN	08609
CN	914.25
AC	
TC	Roma
DC	
D	

2481

16557

26 Feb 1958